Persona ls

Interpretive Essays in World Civilizations
Volume I

Personalities and Problems

Interpretive Essays in World Civilizations

VOLUME I

Ken Wolf

Murray State University

Illustrations by John Stephen Hatton

McGraw-Hill, Inc.

New York St. Louis San Francisco Auckland Bogotá Caracas
Lisbon London Madrid Mexico City Milan Montreal New Delhi
San Juan Singapore Sydney Tokyo Toronto

This book was set in Palatino by The Clarinda Company.
The editors were Pamela Gordon and Joseph F. Murphy;
the production supervisor was Leroy A. Young.
The cover was designed by Circa '86.
R. R. Donnelley & Sons Company was printer and binder.

PERSONALITIES AND PROBLEMS
Interpretive Essays in World Civilizations
Volume I

This book is printed on acid-free paper.

1 2 3 4 5 6 7 8 9 0   DOC   DOC   9 0 9 8 7 6 5 4 3

ISBN 0-07-071343-X

Library of Congress Cataloging-in-Publicaton Data

Wolf, Ken, (date).
    Personalities and problems: interpretive essays in world
civilizations / Ken Wolf.
        p.   cm.
    Includes bibliographical references.
    ISBN 0-07-071343-X (v. 1)
    1. Civilization—History.   2. Biography.   I. Title.
CB69.W63   1994
909—dc20   93-27176

About the Author

KEN WOLF is professor of History and coordinator of the Interdisciplinary World Civilization course at Murray State University in Murray, Kentucky, where he has taught since 1969. He was born in Davenport, Iowa, and received his B.A. degree from St. Ambrose College (1965) and his M.A. and Ph.D in History from the University of Notre Dame (1966, 1972). Professor Wolf helped design Murray State's required World Civilization course and has taught it since its inception. He also teaches German History and Development of Historical Thinking on a regular basis. Professor Wolf has published articles on European nationalism, historiography, intellectual history, and the teaching of history in *The Journal of the History of Ideas, The International Encyclopedia of Social Sciences–Biographical Supplement, Teaching History*, the *Illinois Quarterly*, and *The Journal of Kentucky Studies*. An article on teaching history through the use of biographical studies will appear in 1994 in the *AHA Perspectives*. For five years (1987–1991), Professor Wolf served as one of two deans of the Kentucky Governor's Scholars Program, a state-sponsored summer enrichment program for 700 high-achieving, rising high school seniors. He was selected as a Pew Faculty Fellow International Affairs for 1993–1994. He is married with three children, Kevin, Christine, and Becky. His wife, Deanna, is a social worker.

To my family (Deanna, Kevin, Cris, Becky)
and
To the Students, Faculty, and Staff of
the Kentucky Governor's Scholars Program,
1987–1991

For helping me give meaning
to the phrase "life-long learning."

Contents

Preface

Dear Reader:

The people you meet in these pages illustrate the richness and variety of human history from the earliest civilizations to the seventeenth century AD. The personalities range from one of the key figures in the creation of what we call the Judeo-Christian tradition, Moses, to one of the strongest rulers of modern China, Kangxi. If history is the study of human beings who make it, *Personalities and Problems* is an introduction to world civilizations which focuses upon some of the most interesting men and women which the written records of these civilizations allow us to meet. This book assumes no previous knowledge of history; it does assume that the lives of exciting people have a certain magic which captures our attention across the boundaries of space and time.

But most of you know that history is more (sometimes less) than the study of interesting people. If all the interesting historical figures were included in our history texts, the books would be too large to carry, much less read. The people we choose to include in our histories must also be considered interesting or important—by someone. Whether great in the traditional textbook sense of the term or not, each of these personalities was included in this work because I found them interesting and thought their lives could help you better understand some of the issues which historians and other scholars have struggled with in their teaching, research, and writing. Before you can assess their importance for yourselves, it will be helpful for you to begin to classify or organize them.

Eight of the people you will meet in these pages were primarily political leaders—people such as Hammurabi, Asoka, Constantine, Irene, and Genghis Khan. Another seven were primarily thinkers and/or religious leaders; this list includes Moses, Zoroaster, Buddha, Mahavira, Diogenes, Desiderius Erasmus, and Martin Luther. You will also meet four men best described as explorers: Marco Polo, Ibn Battuta, Prince Henry, and Zheng He.

Putting people in such broad categories is, of course, only one way to describe them—and not necessarily the best way. For one thing, in history as in life, people have a way of breaking through our neat categories. Moses, for example, was both a religious leader and a ruler of his people. Men such as Asoka, Constantine, and Julian were also rulers who tried to influence the religious lives of their people. In the period before 1500 AD, in particular, it is very difficult to separate religion and politics. In a larger sense, this book is interdisciplinary; its author is committed to the idea that whatever lines we might draw between subjects in schools, we cannot understand human beings adequately if we separate their political behavior from their religious beliefs, their social position, or their economic concerns.

A second way of classifying people is to ask about the nature and extent of the impact they made on their society. Some, like Hammurabi and Mansa Musa, were important because their actions reflected the dominant values of their society. Others, such as Martin Luther, were significant because they challenged those values. Occasionally we find people who both reflected the beliefs of their time and place and tried to change the way people thought about the world. The Chinese mariner Zheng He did not change the direction of Chinese history in the fifteenth century, but his voyages of exploration offer a fascinating look at what might have been. His counterpart, Prince Henry of Portugal, both reflected European attitudes toward overseas exploration and, by his work, helped Europeans become even more outward-looking. The Greek Cynic Diogenes and his Indian counterpart, the religious reformer Mahavira, challenged people in their respective societies to live up to the standards they professed.

These are only two ways of classifying the personalities in world history. As you read these essays, I invite you to devise some of your own. Your determination of what makes an individual a success or a failure, admirable or deplorable, will be based upon your personal values. I ask only that you also consider the times in which these individuals lived as well as the problems they faced. If you consider both their problems and the values which they brought to bear in trying to solve them, you will begin the process of thinking historically. You will become historically minded.

To help you with this task, all of these personalities are presented to you in relation to a particular issue or issues which they had to face or which their careers raise for us—as thoughtful citizens of an increasingly interdependent world. These issues—noted by the questions which begin each essay—include such things as the role of religion as a social force, the problems faced by female leaders in male-dominated societies, and the way the structures and values of a society affect the way people feel about contact with other cultures. Also, in all but one case (that of the incomparable Genghis Khan), each personality is paired with a contemporary or near-contemporary who had to face a similar problem or deal with a similar issue either in the same civilization or country or in another one. These pairings are often cross-cultural and should help you understand that human problems really do transcend the boundaries of race, creed, or nation. When we begin to see that individuals as different as Kangxi and Louis XIV had to face similar problems in creating a strong dynastic state, we can appreciate the fact that our history is world history and not only a history of individual nations or even civilizations.

Historical greatness, then, is not just a matter of how talented we are (or how lucky) but also a matter of when and where we live. History helps make us as surely as we help make history. If this book challenges you to think about just how and why this happens, it will have served its purpose.

Because this book assumes no prior knowledge of history, or even prior college-level work, I use brackets [ ] to define terms which might be unfamiliar to a beginning student. You also should know that each chapter is designed to stand independently; chapters need not be read in order. You can start at any point and read in either direction, after checking with your teacher and the course syllabus, of course! Finally, if you or your teacher think that some personalities are left out who should be included or some are included who should be left out, please write to me at the address listed on page xvi. As you might imagine, it has been difficult to balance the three goals of this work: interesting people, important issues, and useful cross-cultural comparisons. If, God and the publisher willing, *Personalities and Problems* goes into a second edition, I would be pleased to receive suggestions of people who ought to be included or omitted. Your comments will be taken seriously.

Personalities and Problems would not have been written without the generous moral and financial support of my colleagues at Murray State University. A sabbatical leave provided by these colleagues and financial support provided by the Murray State Committee on Institutional Studies and Research gave me the time to complete the book. I am particularly grateful to Joseph Cartwright, who suggested and supported the idea; to students Albert Reid, Ann Henry, Nick Greenwell, Rick Jobs and Cheri Harper Greer, whose bibliographic work, notetaking, proofreading, and word processing saved me many hours; to current and former Murray State colleagues Charlotte Beahan, Bill Schell, Mel Page, James Hammack, Wayne Beasley, Joe Fuhrmann, Burt Folsom, Terry Strieter, Roy Hatton, Hughie Lawson, Ken Harrell, Roy Finkenbine, and other readers, at Murray State and elsewhere; to the hardworking Reference and Inter-library Loan staff at Murray State; to Robert Blackey, California State University at San Bernardino; Nancy Erickson, Erskine College; and Thomas Keefe, Appalachian State University for their helpful reviews; and to History Editor Pam Gordon at McGraw-Hill, who did excellent editing and knew when and how to be encouraging as well as firm when asking for revisions. I would also like to particularly thank John Stephen Hatton for rendering all of the text art. Finally, I appreciate the many teachers and students in the Interdisciplinary World Civilizations course at Murray State who "field-tested" these essays in their classes over the past ten years. Any errors which you find are my responsibility, not to be blamed on any of the above, who often tried unsuccessfully to save me from myself. All of my colleagues do join me, however, in hoping that this work offers you both pleasant reading and intellectual excitement.

Sincerely,

Ken Wolf

Department of History
Murray State University
Murray, KY 42071

Personalities and Problems

Interpretive Essays in World Civilizations

Volume I

CHAPTER 1

Hammurabi and Moses: Law as a Mirror of Civilization

What do the laws of a society tell us about the lives and beliefs of the people who write, enforce, and obey those laws?

Early civilizations were both fragile and gradual. We often make lists of their qualities as if they were chemical compounds or recipes: Take several Neolithic farming villages and a river valley; add a group of nomadic herdsmen; stir briskly with bronze weapons. Blend in language, cities, writing, a system of class differentiation with warriors and priests at the head of the list, and simmer until a civilization emerges. Garnish with trade and conquest before serving.

Of course, it did not happen that way. The ideas, customs, and material things which constituted early civilizations came together slowly over many centuries. Only after the fact, when the cities or settlements with their kings, priests, beliefs, shops, and soldiers were all in place, do we speak of a particular civilization. And this complex social, political, and economic creation was both strong and weak—strong enough to engage in wars of conquest, weak enough to be destroyed by the death of a powerful leader, or by a famine caused by a drop of two degrees in the average annual mean temperature.

While it lasted, each great early civilization was held together by power and traditions: the power of political and social elites, and the traditions embodied in the great religious and philosophical value systems that mark all major civilizations.

These traditions give meaning to political and social institutions—to family life, education, government, and the marketplace. Though it is not always mentioned (because it is taken for granted),

1

the power and traditions of any society or civilization are reflected in its laws.

We see such reflections in two early, but very different, civilizations in the ancient Near East: the Babylonian and the Hebrew. The first developed in the early part of the second millennium BC in the Tigris and Euphrates valley, while the second came together in the thirteenth century BC when Moses led the Hebrew people out of Egypt east into the Sinai Desert. The most famous ruler of the Babylonians was Hammurabi, who ruled from 1792 to 1750 BC. After long wars in which he conquered the older Sumerian cities such as Larsa, Erech, and Ur in the southern part of Mesopotamia, Hammurabi published a list of 300 laws by carving them into a black basalt pillar seven feet high and two feet in diameter which he erected near the site of the modern city of Baghdad in Iraq. Moses claimed to have received at least some of his laws directly from God while the Hebrews wandered through the Sinai Desert after leaving Egypt. Nearly all the Hebrew laws are recorded in their holy book, the Torah (the Law), which makes up the first five books of the Hebrew Bible, or Old Testament.

Although both Hammurabi and Moses are famous as lawgivers, scholars are quick to point out that Hammurabi's famous "Code" was not really a modern collection of laws, nor were the laws in it particularly new. The same is true of the "laws of Moses" found in the Torah. In both cases the laws and traditions ascribed to these men were derived in part from earlier traditions. Hammurabi's Code is a collection of time-honored Mesopotamian legal principles developed earlier in the Sumerian cities. Many of the laws in the Mosaic, or Covenant, Code of the Hebrews found in Exodus borrow heavily from Hammurabi's Code; others, especially those in Deuteronomy, were developed in the late seventh century BC long after the Hebrews had left the desert and established themselves in Palestine. Although Hammurabi and Moses were real people, their names became symbols of the traditions and values of their respective civilizations; Moses, in particular, became a nucleus around which legends formed.

It was easy for legends to form because so little was known about the lives of Hammurabi and Moses. Hammurabi was an active ruler who spent the last fourteen years of his reign in continuous warfare attempting to control the people along the Euphrates River. He wanted "to make justice appear in the land, to destroy the evil and the wicked [so] that the strong might not oppress the weak."[1] We know the familiar story of Moses told in Exodus: how the infant was found by the Pharaoh's daughter in a basket made of bulrushes (the same story is told of an early Sumerian king); how the adult Moses killed an Egyptian, then fled to Midian, where he became a shepherd and the son-in-law of a Midian priest; how God called him from a burning bush to lead his people out of Egypt; and how he did this, probably during the reign of Pharaoh Rameses II (1304–1237 BC).

It is interesting that Moses is presented throughout this book as a fully human person on whom God "imposes" His will. This reflects the unique relationship between God and humankind in the Hebrew tradition. The Hebrew God was so different from humans that his image could not be drawn nor his name spoken or written in full except on special occasions, and yet he made agreements with a people who were clearly weak and fallible. Other ancient peoples, unlike the Hebrews, often depicted their gods in human or animal form rather than seeing humans as made in the image of God. The book of Exodus also shows Moses to be a man passionately concerned with social justice and what we call today "national liberation." No nonscriptural source of that time speaks of him, and so our knowledge of Moses is limited by what scriptures tell us about Moses as the leader, prophet, and liberator of his people.[2]

The actual lives of these men are less important than what the laws ascribed to them tell about the lifestyle of their peoples. The laws of Hammurabi as well as those in the Old Testament tell us much about what the Babylonians and Hebrews considered important; reading them allows us to look into their law courts, temples, businesses, homes, and even their hearts and minds. We can see how their values differed from ours, as well as how they were similar. In the final analysis, the laws of the Babylonians, a commercial, city-oriented people who worshipped many gods, differed significantly from those of the Hebrews, a pastoral people who worshipped a single deity called Yahweh.

Initially, however, the similarities between the laws of these two peoples are more striking than the differences. The most famous feature of Hammurabi's Code is its emphasis on the law of retaliation *(lex talionis)*. This demands, in the words of laws 196 and 200, that "if a man has put out the eye of a free man, they shall put out his eye. . . . If a man knocks out the tooth of a free man equal in rank to himself, they shall knock out his tooth." Law 209 states: "If a man strikes the daughter of a free man and causes her to lose the fruit of her womb, he shall pay 10 shekels of silver." In the oldest Hebrew laws, those of the Covenant Code found in Exodus, we read: "When men strive together, and hurt a woman with child, so that there is a miscarriage . . . the one who hurt her shall be fined, according as the woman's husband shall lay upon him; and he shall pay as the judge determines. If any harm follows, then you shall give life for life, eye for eye, tooth for tooth, hand for hand, burn for burn, wound for wound, stripe for stripe."[3] In this case, the Hebrew laws seem to be a clear summary and paraphrase of the earlier Babylonian statutes.

Hebrew and Mesopotamian laws dealing with lying are also similar, the law in Hammurabi's Code reading crisply: "If a man has come forward in a case to bear witness to a felony and then has not proved the statement he has made, if that case is a capital one, that man shall be put to death." In Deuteronomy 19:16–19, someone who wished to accuse another of wrongdoing has to "appear before the Lord," that is, the priests and judges, who "shall inquire diligently, and if the witness . . . has accused his brother falsely, then you shall do to him as he had meant to do to his brother. . . ." Two verses later, we find the lex talionis repeated again: "Your eye shall not pity; it shall be life for life, eye for eye, tooth for tooth, hand for hand, foot for foot." Hammurabi's laws and those of Moses dealing with people being placed in slavery as payment for debts are also similar, although the Hebrews required such people to serve six years in order to earn their freedom while the Babylonians specified three; interestingly, in both cases a man could place his wife or child in temporary servitude in payment for his debt.[4]

In the area of marriage law, there are again similarities between the laws of Hammurabi and those of Moses. In both societies, controlling sexual relations was very important. This is understandable if we realize that here, as in most early societies, marriage was, first and foremost, a legal contract aimed at the production of children and the safeguarding of property rights for both parties. A Babylonian woman brought to her marriage a dowry which was designed to protect her and her children from arbitrary action by her husband more than it was intended to enrich him. This is clear from several divorce laws which state that in case of divorce, sanctioned if a woman were barren, the husband "shall give her money to the value of her bridal gift and shall make good to her the dowry which she brought from her father's house." Hebrew divorce law was less protective of the wife. A man could divorce his wife if he had "found some indecency in her"; he had only to "write her a bill of divorce and put it in her hand and send her out of his house."[5] In both societies, a barren woman could avoid divorce by allowing her husband to have children by a "slave-girl." This practice, followed by the Hebrew patriarch Abraham and described in the book of Genesis, shows the importance of childbearing. Laws allowing children by slave women also indicate how Hammurabi used earlier Sumerian traditions, since Abraham came from this area south of Babylonia and lived several centuries before Hammurabi. The importance of properly caring for children in Hammurabi's society is clear in several laws which gave a woman the right to live with another man ("enter another man's house") if her husband had left her for an extended period of time without adequate support. The husband, who might have been a prisoner of war or on a business trip that took longer than planned, did have the right to reclaim his family when he returned. However, if the woman had been amply provided for and still entered another man's house, the judge was required to "convict that woman and cast her into the water."[6]

This last provision raises the question of sexual fidelity in marriage, a problem as old as humankind and one that people in traditional societies had to deal with because important questions of inheritance were at stake. Both societies were generally harsh in punishing infidelity. "If a woman has procured the death of her husband on account of another man, they shall impale that woman," reads law 153 in Hammurabi's Code. "If a man is found lying with the wife of another man, both of them shall die," according to Deuteronomy 22:22. As we might expect, each society condemned not only adultery but also homosexuality, violating "betrothed virgins," and incest. In Hammurabi's Code, a man was banished for having carnal relations with his daughter and could be "cast into the water" for "lying in the bosom" of his son's betrothed. A son and his mother were burned for sleeping together after the father/husband's death. Hebrew law included long lists of persons whose "nakedness" was not to be "uncovered." The list included all members of the immediate family as well as aunts, uncles, sisters-in-law, half brothers and sisters, grandchildren, and, finally, for good measure, "any beast."[7]

This prohibition against bestiality highlights a difference between Hebrew and Babylonian marriage laws. Unlike the subjects of Hammurabi, the people of Moses were concerned with more than just keeping lines of inheritance clear. In both Leviticus and Deuteronomy, there is a concern with morality and holiness as well as with property rights. Many of the statements in Deuteronomy end with the words "so you shall purge the evil from Israel." Violations of these laws are called "defilements" in Leviticus and are considered abominable because they affect the community spiritually as well as socially; Yahweh would look unfavorably upon the Hebrew community if such individual defilements were allowed to exist unpunished.

Differences between the laws of Hammurabi and those of Moses become clearer as we look at statutes relating to agriculture. Babylonian lands were honeycombed with irrigation canals and dikes whose upkeep was crucial to the welfare of the entire Mesopotamian area. Therefore it is not surprising to read that if a farmer was lax in maintaining the irrigation canals on his land, thus allowing water to break through a dike and flood a neighbor's field, he had to replace the lost crop. If he could not afford to do this, "he and his goods" would be sold to pay the debt to his neighbor. Hammurabi's Code also assumed that most land was rented out and provided very specific protections for the landlord if the rented land was not properly cultivated. Hebrew society in Palestine, by contrast, was largely pastoral with few large cities. Most land was owned by individuals and not rented out, and the people, in general, were poorer. The law of Moses, therefore, says little about landlord-tenant relationships but much about the responsibility of farmers toward the poor. Land was to lie fallow every seven years so that the poor could gather the residue from such fields, orchards, or vineyards. The Hebrews were also told not to clear their fields or vineyards entirely, but to leave a strip around the edge "for the poor and for the sojourner."[8] No such humanitarian injunctions are found in Hammurabi's Code, indicating not only that Babylonian society was more centralized, urban, wealthy, and highly structured, but also that the Hebrews consciously tried to temper justice with mercy. Hammurabi's Code also naturally reflects the complex, differentiated social structure of the densely populated Mesopotamian region. Slaves are one of three groups of people mentioned in the

Code. There were two other major classes, *awilum*, or free men, and *muskenum*, or those dependent upon another. Men in the last group were sometimes called "villeins" or "subjects"; we might compare them with modern sharecroppers or tenant farmers. They were clearly submissive to others, either to their upper-class landlord or to the king—since much of the land was owned directly by the government. The eyes and teeth of villeins were not worth as much as those of free men. Law 201, for example, specified that one who knocked out the tooth of a villein pay one-third maneh of silver; law 198 required that the broken bone or the eye of a villein be paid for with one maneh of silver.[9] While this was a considerable sum (slightly over a pound of silver), it was better than losing an eye.

Justice, therefore, had a clear relationship to class standing in Hammurabi's kingdom. Class differences even affected the cost of medical services. Surgery cost a free man ten shekels (two to three ounces of silver), a villein five, and a slave only two—if the patient lived. If the patient was a free man and died during surgery, the surgeon could lose his hand; if the victim of poor surgery was only a slave, the surgeon had only to replace the man with another.[10] These penalties, class bias aside, were deliberate attempts to encourage efficiency. And in a society where a single broken dike, bad harvest, or unprotected city wall could mean disaster, harsh measures taken to ensure efficiency were understandable.

These penalties for inefficiency were severe in this society where the government's attempts to control daily life rivaled those of modern authoritarian states. Consider the alewife who would be put to death under law 109 if she failed to turn in felons who frequented her alehouse; or the builder (law 229) who knew he would be executed if a house he built fell down, killing the householder. Efficiency was important to the shipbuilder who was forced by law to guarantee his work.[11]

The Hebrew Torah, on the other hand, has no such rules since the seminomadic pastoral people of Palestine did not have commercial house builders, or a maritime industry. Hammurabi had inscribed dozens of laws on his pillar which have no parallels in the laws of Moses: sixteen laws defining the duties of soldiers, constables, and tax collectors; eleven dealing with physicians; twelve regulating the activity of merchants (including wine sellers); six each concerning the obligations of house builders and boatmen; one dealing with the collision of ships; and over a dozen regulating wages and prices.[12]

These last—those regulating wages and prices—are detailed and famous. Wages for tailors, carpenters, potters, jewelers, blacksmiths, leatherworkers, and bricklayers were all fixed by law. Modern economists frown on wage and price fixing, claiming that it stifles private initiative, encourages black market activity, or, at best, causes shortages of goods and services. While we do not know how strictly the wage and price laws in Hammurabi's Code were followed, we do know that the Babylonian economy had a large amount of state control but also a strong "private sector." Since much land was owned directly by the king, many of the villeins or tenant farmers were, in effect, government employees. Yet the Babylonians developed a form of capitalism "by providing interest as an incentive for investing capital." One section of the Code limits the interest rate to twenty percent on loans of grain or silver.[13] Hammurabi even wrote measures regulating conduct among business partners, merchants, and their salespeople, and between grain bin owners and their customers.

We might naturally ask how such elaborate laws were enforced. Soldiers and police can try to enforce laws, whether they are fair or not, but for laws to last as long as these it is necessary for decisions of judges to be backed by some moral authority which both parties in court can respect. No premodern legal system worked without religious sanction, and when we look at the authority behind the laws in the Babylonian and Hebrew civilizations we can better understand why the Old Testament laws had a more profound moral effect on human history than those devised by the Mesopotamians and codified by Hammurabi.

Earlier we noticed that the Hebrew laws concerning agriculture were marked by a humanitarian emphasis not found in their Babylonian counterparts. This concern for the less fortunate is clear throughout the Torah. In the earlier laws found in Exodus, the followers of Moses were told twice: "You shall not wrong a stranger or oppress him, for you were strangers in the land of Egypt." One of these passages continues: "You shall not afflict any widow or orphan. If you do afflict them, and they cry out to me, I will surely hear their cry; and my wrath will burn, and I will kill you with the sword, and your wives shall become widows and your children fatherless." Later, in Leviticus, the Hebrews are warned not to oppress their neighbors, including the deaf and the blind, and to "not be partial to the poor or defer to the great." In Deuteronomy 10:17–19 the sanction for all of these warnings becomes clear:

> For the Lord your God is God of gods and Lord of lords, the great, the mighty, and the terrible God, who is not partial and takes no bribes. He executes justice for the fatherless and the widow, and loves the sojourner, giving him food and clothing. Love the sojourner therefore; for you were sojourners in the land of Egypt.[14]

From at least the time of Moses, the Hebrews believed in a single all-powerful God, Yahweh, the "God of gods and Lord of lords." In their early history the Hebrews accepted the fact that other people worshipped other gods; they simply believed that their god Yahweh was more powerful. This belief, sometimes called henotheism, evolved into full-scale monotheism, the belief that there exists only one god for everyone. But even before Moses, the Hebrews believed that their laws, starting with those embodied in the Ten Commandments and ending with a host of regulations governing the details of everyday behavior, were given to them directly by Yahweh. And as these passages from the Torah indicate, Yahweh not only sought justice for his people; he loved them as well.

Nowhere in Hammurabi's Code, for example, do we find a law like the Torah's telling a businessman not to charge interest when he loans money to the poor and adding: "If you take your neighbor's garment in pledge, you shall restore it to him before the sun goes down; for that is his only covering, it is his mantle . . . in what else shall he sleep?" And, as usual in the Torah, this injunction is followed by the enforcing statement: "And if he cries to me, I will hear, for I am compassionate."[15] In other places the word "compassionate" is replaced with such words as "faithful," "just," or "holy."

Of course, Hammurabi's Code, despite the modern sound of many of its provisions, was not a "secular" document. Hammurabi himself clearly believed in the existence of the gods and in a moral universe which their actions sustained—with his help. He ended his Code by asking the gods to curse anyone who would change his work. He asked Ninlil, "the great mother," to destroy the land, ruin the people, and "pour out the life-blood" of any future ruler who would change the Code. Shamash, "the great judge of heaven and earth," was called upon not only to kill such a man but "to make his ghost thirst for water in the world below." Ishtar, "the lady of battle and conflict," was asked to leave the armies of anyone bold enough to change the laws "a heap of corpses on the plain."[16]

Although Hammurabi ended by calling upon the gods, his Code is remembered not as a great moral document but rather as one of the first great legal statements of the notion that the injured should receive compensation and that harsh punishments should be used as a deterrent to crime. These Babylonian principles found their way into Hebrew law and later into other legal systems; they are found in the laws of many modern nations.

Though they did borrow heavily from the Mesopotamians, the Hebrews passed on a different legacy. While the Mosaic code is followed in detail today by only a small number of Orthodox Jews, the general moral principles of the Torah, especially the Ten Commandments and concern for the poor and oppressed, have become an integral part of the laws and political practices of many Western nations. Just as some of our modern civil laws giving people the right to sue for personal injuries might be said to have descended from Babylonian laws, so too do many of our laws protecting the poor remind us of the principles of the Old Testament.

Perhaps this is why, even today, when we hear the phrase "an eye for an eye and a tooth for a tooth," we "know" it came from "the Bible." Given all the borrowing he did in putting together his Code, Hammurabi would probably understand—and let us escape with only a small curse for misunderstanding the origin of the *lex talionis*.

Notes

1. G. R. Driver and John C. Miles, editors, *The Babylonian Laws*, Volume II (Oxford: Clarendon Press, 1952), 7. This complete annotated translation of Hammurabi's laws is hereafter referred to as *Laws*.
2. In addition to the many encyclopedia articles on Moses, see André Neher, *Men of Wisdom: Moses and the Vocation of the Jewish People*, trans. by Irene Marinoff (New York: Harper and Row, 1959); Martin Noth, *A History of Pentateuchal Traditions*, trans. and introduced by Bernhard W. Anderson (Englewood Cliffs, NJ: Prentice-Hall, 1972), 156–174; Elie Wiesel, "Moses: Portrait of a Leader," in *Messengers of God: Biblical Portraits and Legends* (New York: Random House, 1976), 174–205.
3. Driver and Miles, *Laws*, II, 78–79; Exodus 22:22–25. All citations from the Old Testament are taken from *The Oxford Annotated Bible*, Revised Standard Version (New York: Oxford University Press, 1962).
4. Driver and Miles, *Laws*, II, 15, 48–49; Deuteronomy 19:16–19; Deuteronomy 15:12–18; Exodus 21:2–11.

5. Driver and Miles, *Laws*, II, 55; Deuteronomy 24:1.
6. Driver and Miles, *Laws*, II, 53–57. Being "cast into the water" in Hammurabi's Code refers to a trial in which a defendant would be bound and thrown into the river: if he or she floated, he or she was deemed innocent; if the person sank, he or she was considered guilty—as well as dead, verdict and sentence being determined nearly simultaneously.
7. Driver and Miles, *Laws*, II, 57, 61; Leviticus 18:6–23. The differences between Hammurabi's Code and Hebrew laws dealing with chastity, marriage, and divorce are also summarized in George Barton, *Archeology and the Bible* (Philadelphia: American Sunday School Union, 1916), 326–329.
8. Driver and Miles, *Laws*, II, 27–31; Exodus 23:10–11, Leviticus 19:9, Deuteronomy 24:19–22.
9. Driver and Miles, *Laws*, II, 77.
10. *Ibid.*, 79, 81.
11. *Ibid.*, 45, 83, 85.
12. *Ibid.*, 21–27, 79–81, 43–45, 83–85, 89–93; see also Barton, *Archeology and the Bible*, 316–317, 322, 336–339.
13. Cyrus H. Gordon, editor, *Hammurabi's Code: Quaint or Forward-Looking?* (New York: Holt, Rinehart and Winston, 1957), 8.
14. Exodus 22:21–27; 23: 9; Leviticus 19:13–15; Deuteronomy 10:17–19.
15. Exodus 22:25–27.
16. Driver and Miles, *Laws*, II, 95–107.

Further Reading

BARTON, GEORGE. *Archeology and the Bible* (Philadelphia: American Sunday School Union, 1916). Old but includes wonderfully succinct comparisons.

GAAD, CYRIL. "Hammurabi: The End of His Dynasty," in *Cambridge Ancient History*, Third Edition (Cambridge: Cambridge University Press, 1975), Volume II. Good, short account of the man.

GORDON, CYRUS H., editor. *Hammurabi's Code: Quaint or Forward-Looking?* (New York: Holt, Rinehart and Winston, 1957). Scholars debate the role and value of the Code.

NEHER, ANDRÉ. *Men of Wisdom: Moses and the Vocation of the Jewish People*, trans. by Irene Marinoff (New York: Harper and Row, 1959). Insight into the man and his mission.

CHAPTER 2

Zoroaster and Buddha: Explaining Suffering

Why does evil exist in the world? What are the different "Western" and "Eastern" ways of answering this question, and what are some implications of these answers for our understanding of world history?

Why do people suffer? Why does evil exist in the world? These questions, asked by millions of people throughout human history, have helped inspire most of humanity's great philosophies and religions. While the questions are simple, the answers which thinkers have given to them are often complicated—and certainly varied.

During the sixth century before the birth of Christ, several important attempts were made to explain suffering and evil. The Chinese sage Kung Fuzi (Confucius, 551–479 BC) believed that suffering was caused by people's failure to love and respect one another properly. The system of ethics he devised to remedy this lack of mutual respect helped mold Chinese civilization for over 2000 years. In this same, very creative, sixth century, other men offered religious answers to the problem of suffering. Two notable seekers of truth were Zarathustra (ca. 628–551 BC), a Persian nobleman and founder of a religion known as Zoroastrianism, and Siddhartha Gautama (ca. 560–480 BC), an Indian known later as the Buddha and founder of Buddhism. These two men offered specific and very different answers to our questions about suffering and evil. Their ideas are also worthy of our attention because their respective philosophies represent two ways of looking at the world—one of which can be called "Western" and the other "Eastern."

It may seem unusual to refer to Zarathustra or Zoroaster (the Greek version of his name by which he is usually known) as a Westerner since he was born not far from the modern Iranian capital of

Teheran in what many today call the Middle East. Yet in Zoroaster's day, the Greek cities were on the western fringe of the civilized world and the Persian Empire itself was considered the East by those in the Mediterranean world. Zoroaster was probably a priest and a member of the Spitama clan in Persia. His early life was apparently ordinary, but about age twenty he left home (which may have included his three wives and six children) and began to wander the countryside seeking Truth. After ten years of wandering, he had a vision of an angel, Vohu Manah (Good Thought), who told Zoroaster that there was only one God, Ahura Mazda (the Wise Lord), and that Zoroaster was to become his prophet. During the next several years, Zoroaster had other visions in which other messengers of Ahura Mazda appeared to him to reveal God's message. Although the newly anointed prophet began to preach immediately, he was persecuted and defied for ten years. Finally, he converted his cousin Maidhyomah to his new faith. They then journeyed east to Bactria (modern Afghanistan), where Zoroaster won over King Vishtaspa and his court. From this point, Zoroastrianism spread more rapidly among the Aryan peoples in the Persian Empire. At times the new religion was spread by war, and it was during one of these wars, we are told, that the seventy-seven-year-old Zoroaster was killed while tending the sacred fire at an altar.

Though it is hard to know all of Zoroaster's teachings with certainty, since many early writings were lost and his doctrines were greatly changed in later centuries, a series of hymns, or "Gathas," generally thought to be the work of the prophet himself suggest that this man was one of history's first monotheists.[1] While most people at this time believed that there were many gods, Zoroaster declared firmly that Ahura Mazda was the only one. He credited this God with creating the world and all the good things in it; Ahura Mazda wished all to live a life of "pure thought, pure words, and pure deeds," and he judged individuals after their death on how well they had succeeded.[2] Those who followed Truth during their lives would go to heaven, while those who followed the Lie would be sent to hell.

The existence of a hell in Zoroaster's religion tells us, in the words of one scholar, that "although Ahura Mazda is supreme, he is not unopposed." In Zoroastrianism, the Good Spirit, or Spenta Mainyu, analogous to the Holy Spirit in Christianity, is opposed to the Bad Spirit, or Angra Mainyu. This evil spirit is very much like

Satan in traditional Christian theology; he is a "prince of darkness," the very embodiment of lies, cowardice, and all other forms of misery. Ahura Mazda allows people to choose between himself and Angra Mainyu.[3] By their free choice, men and women can both save themselves and also advance the cause of goodness and truth in the world. In the final reckoning, the world would be saved; Ahura Mazda would win a last great victory over the Evil Spirit—even hell would finally come to an end.[4] Humans could bring this final judgment day closer by living a life of goodness and purity and by deeds which spread the goodness of Ahura Mazda in the world in which they lived. The moral life involved struggle and choice—here rather than in the hereafter.

If all this sounds much like the world view preached by Christianity, as well as by Judaism and Islam, for that matter, you should note that many scholars see important connections among these four Western religions. Some believe that the Jews adopted some basic ideas about good and evil, heaven, hell, and final judgment from the disciples of Zoroaster while the Judeans were held captive in Babylon during the sixth century (586–539 BC). These new beliefs were then inherited by Christians and Muslims, both of whom accept basic Hebrew beliefs contained in the Old Testament, or Jewish Bible. This explanation of the Zoroastrian origins of basic Western religious ideas is convenient. Unfortunately, there is no direct evidence that it is true.[5] While similarities clearly exist in the way Zoroaster and the major Western religions explain evil, no one is able to say exactly who took what from whom—or when this happened.

What we can say is that Zoroaster's explanation of evil and suffering, however it may have been modified by his own Persian followers and however it may have been adapted, or even influenced, by the Jews, has had a powerful impact on Western thought. All major Western religions since Zoroaster's day have highly valued four things: (1) the role of the individual person; (2) the material world in which we live; (3) time and human history; (4) the role of a supremely powerful, transcendent Creator God. All four were important in Zoroaster's fight against evil and suffering. Let us briefly examine each in turn.

For Zoroaster, individuals were more than helpless victims of suffering. While he believed in few rituals (veneration of fire as a symbol of truth and of water as a symbol of purity were central ones), Zoroaster did assert that good deeds would be rewarded, and he called upon his followers to be aggressive in resisting evil. One of the most prominent good deeds mentioned in the Gathas is concern for cattle. The Bactrians whom Zoroaster converted were a pastoral people who survived on simple forms of agriculture and on cattle rearing; their enemies were nomadic warriors from the north who often invaded their settlements. Thus it is not surprising that Zoroaster called these tribal horsemen the "followers of the Lie" and declared virtuous any action that promoted agriculture, made the earth more fruitful, or protected sheep or cattle. Good deeds might be simple deeds for sixth-century rural Persians, but virtuous human actions were important to the salvation of the world.

Since human actions were essential for the defeat of evil, the material world where such actions take place was also important. Zoroastrianism, like Judaism, Christianity, and Islam after it, was a world-affirming religion. The battle between Good and Evil was fought on earth, in the human soul but also in the home, field, or shop. Zoroaster did not believe in torturing the flesh, or in other forms of monastic self-denial. His followers were not supposed to escape from the world in order to bring themselves closer to Ahura Mazda; they were to help Ahura Mazda by living a life of virtue in the world.

Given this affirmation of humanity and the world, it is logical that Zoroaster would regard measurement of time as important. Although Zoroastrians do not see God intervening in human history in the ways described in the Old Testament, they do believe that the world and time itself will end with the last judgment or the Final Rehabilitation, as some Zoroastrian scriptures refer to it.[6] In the distant but foreseeable future, the power of the Evil Spirit over man will be ended.

This will happen because of the ultimate power and beneficence of an all-powerful God. However important the ethical choices we must make, Ahura Mazda will have the last word: "In immortality (or eternity) shall the soul of the righteous be joyful, in perpetuity shall be the torments of the Liar. . . . Thine, Mazda, is the Dominion, whereby thou canst give to the right-living poor man the better portion."[7]

In summary, then, evil for Zoroaster was not caused by the omnipotent Supreme Being, but only permitted by him. The Spirit of Evil was a necessary consequence of free choice. If people were to be free, they had to be free to choose evil. But if people could choose evil, they could also choose good. Suffering was caused by Angra Mainyu, aided by his followers on earth; it was painful, but temporary. This explanation has at least two logical flaws: It does not explain why innocent people suffer, nor does it tell us why an all-powerful, good God would give evil such free rein in the first place. These logical flaws have been the subject of intense debate by religious philosophers through the centuries. Judged by the general directness and practical tone of Zoroaster's words in the Gathas, he was not much interested in such metaphysical abstractions. In that respect, at least, he was much like his Indian contemporary Siddhartha Gautama, who otherwise lived in a very different thought world. Gautama's value for us is that he tried to answer just those two questions that Zoroaster left unanswered.

Like Zoroaster, Siddhartha Gautama came from the upper class. His father was ruler of a small state in northeastern India (now Nepal). Gautama's status as a nobleman was important in helping explain why he became interested in the problem of suffering. Although there are many legends about the birth and early life of this young prince, the most frequently repeated one tells us that Siddhartha's father was warned by a Hindu priest that the young man would become a famous religious leader instead of a ruler if he ever became acquainted with old age, illness, death, or the ways of a begging monk. Not wanting this to happen, Siddhartha's father tried to shield him from such things by providing him with a life of luxury. The young prince was married at sixteen and lived in a beautiful palace surrounded by young, beautiful people. One day, so we are told, Siddhartha had to leave the palace grounds and, despite his father's precautions, happened to see an old man. He asked his driver what sort of creature this was and was shocked when the driver explained old age. On three other journeys, he saw an ill person, a corpse, and a wandering monk.

After seeing these things, the sensitive prince determined to leave his fine home, his young wife, and his infant son (religious leaders are often poor family men). For six years, beginning at about age thirty, Gautama wandered through India, attempting to discover truth and tranquility by living the life of an ascetic, one who rejects the pleasures of the flesh, especially eating, in order to better concentrate the mind. After years of severe fasting—one legend has it that the soon-to-be Buddha ate as little as one grain of rice a day for a time—Gautama was no closer to the knowledge he sought. Finally he stopped fasting and sat down under a tree on the banks of a river, vowing to remain there until he understood truth. In the course of one night, according to an early Buddhist scripture, Gautama achieved Enlightenment, a state of mind and soul in which he understood the nature of good and evil and was freed from the temptations and illusions that beset others.

After this awakening, the Buddha (a term that means "awakened or enlightened one") went into the nearest town (modern Benares) and preached his first sermon in a deer park to a handful of his former companions who had left him earlier when he stopped fasting. This Deer Park Sermon sums up the essential message of the Buddha as described in the Four Noble Truths: All existence is suffering; all suffering is caused by craving or desire; suffering can be ended; and the way to end suffering is to follow the Noble Eightfold Path. The steps on this path include: right views, right intentions, right speech, right action, right livelihood, right effort, right mindfulness, and right meditation. Travelers on this path follow a standard moral code which forbids lying, stealing, killing, and other forms of violence and combine this with an emphasis on meditation designed to help the individual gain *panna*, or wisdom.

What was this wisdom which the Buddha preached throughout northern India until his death forty-five years after his Enlightenment? Although Buddhism has become a major world religion in Asia in the twenty-five centuries since Buddha's death, it is important to distinguish—just as it was in the case of Zoroaster—the original teachings of Gautama from those of his followers, many of whom tried to turn him into a god, the Lord Buddha. This is not something Gautama would have appreciated, for it was a fundamental conviction of his that humans, and not any divine power, were responsible for evil. Buddha did not speak of God or sin. Evil came simply from people's desires for things they could not obtain. God or gods do not punish us; we punish ourselves by our own greed and craving. Because of this very human explanation of evil, the Buddha has been called an atheist by some; for example, by the main character in Gore Vidal's novel *Creation*.[8] But although Buddha may not have been religious in the sense in which most of us understand this term, he did share a goal with Zoroaster and other religious teachers: the overcoming of death. The way he proposed we do this reveals his debt to Hinduism as well as the basic difference between his philosophy and that of Zoroaster.

All Hindus believe in reincarnation. The individual soul is re-born, or reincarnated, many times before it reaches release *(moshka)*, or salvation. Good actions cause one to be reborn higher in the so-cial or caste system; bad actions cause one to be reborn in a lower social caste, or perhaps even as an animal. This happened accord-ing to law, not grace: one's deeds *(karma)* advanced or retarded one's attempt to escape from the wheel, or circle, of life. The goal of Hinduism is to eliminate death by stopping rebirth. Emancipation comes for the individual when his or her soul is merged into the world-soul *(brahman)* and is no longer reborn. Buddha accepted this basic teaching. His philosophy differed from that of classical Hin-duism by making salvation (which he called *nirvana*) accessible to all, not just to members of the higher castes of priests, warriors, and merchants. He also espoused a "middle way" between extreme physical self-denial and excessive attachment to the world.

And Buddha's "middle way" is really one of great psychological sophistication—if we accept his suppositions. If we believe with him that the physical, material world is really one of illusion *(maya)* and that everything that exists is impermanent, it makes sense for us to stop craving or desiring material things. But Buddha went even fur-ther. He said that the individual soul or self was also impermanent. Therefore, to reach Nirvana, or ultimate tranquility, and end all suf-fering, one had to "extinguish" the individual ego or self. One stu-dent of Buddhism explains this mystifying process by which an indi-vidual self is "extinguished" and enters Nirvana as follows:

> Imagine an illimitable ocean in which there are innumerable vials [bottles]. Each vial is filled with sea-water belonging to that very ocean and each is composed of a substance that gradually thick-ens or dissolves in response to circumstances. Under suitable con-ditions, it dissolves altogether, whereupon the water it contains becomes indistinguishable from the rest of the ocean. Not one drop of water ceases to exist; all that is lost is its apparent sepa-rateness. In this analogy, the water in each vial represents a so-called individual being and the gradual thickening or dissolving vial symbolizes his mental and physical characteristics . . . [which are] born of Avidya (greed) and nourished by the force of karma. . . . Once [these] have been dissolved, the being's "sepa-rate" identity ceases.[9]

How different all this was from the teachings of Zoroaster! Buddha believed struggle of any kind was part of the problem; men and women had to "let go" of attachments to all things and all ideas (even to the idea of nonattachment) in order to be Enlightened. The Persian prophet, on the other hand, saw struggle—as long as it was against the Evil One—as a positive good. Buddha, like many of his Hindu predecessors, saw the material world as a place to escape from; for Zoroaster it was a place where the salvation of each individual had to be worked out by life-enriching, world-blessing deeds. The single biggest difference between these two seers was the way they understood time. Zoroastrians had but one chance to achieve heaven and avoid hell; Buddhists could take many lifetimes to reach Nirvana. Zoroaster, like all Western religious leaders, saw time as finite. Man and the world would end, either sooner or later, but at some foreseeable point. Buddhists and Hindus saw time as virtually endless; for them the universe was created and re-created over vast periods of time known to Buddhists as *kalpas*. When someone asked Buddha how long a *kalpa* was, he asked the questioner to imagine a man wiping a mighty mountain peak once each century with a handkerchief. That mountain would be worn away before a *kalpa* had passed.[10]

We can imagine these two famous teachers engaging in a debate. Buddha would smile tranquilly while pointing out to Zoroaster that his God, Ahura Mazda, was playfully cruel in giving men only one chance at salvation. Zoroaster, who disliked paradoxes as much as Buddha enjoyed them, would sternly charge the Buddha with being plainly silly in denying the reality of the material world. The two would agree only that men and women ought to live a good life, avoiding evil so as to achieve salvation. On *how* to do this, there would be fundamental, dare we say eternal, disagreement.

Of course, a debate such as this could never have taken place, even if the Buddha had lived closer to Zoroaster and had not been nine years old when the Persian leader died. Debating itself is a Western device; it assumes that Truth can be discovered through rational discourse. Buddha would have found debating itself silly, for ultimate Truth could only be discovered, he was convinced, through what we call intuition and meditation. Metaphysical speculation and rational argument were of little value to him.

Much of the history of what we call Eastern civilizations makes more sense to us if we understand the values of the Buddha and his followers. The lack of emphasis that many Eastern countries have historically placed on material progress, for example, makes greater sense if we understand Buddhism. The fact that Western nations were the first to pursue material progress and industrialization aggressively also follows logically from the world view of Zoroaster. If you find, however, on finishing this essay, that the tenets of Zoroaster make more sense to you than do those of the Buddha— but if at the same time you are intrigued, even strangely attracted, by the psychologic of Buddha's view of the way to eliminate evil— be thankful! Living in the interdependent world of the late twentieth century, you have more paths to Truth open to you than could be found in the wildest dreams of either Zoroaster or Buddha.

Notes

1. The fourteenth-century (BC) Egyptian Pharaoh Akhenaten and the thirteenth-century Hebrew leader Moses are both examples of monotheists before Zoroaster.
2. Rustom Masani, *Zoroastrianism: The Religion of the Good Life* (New York: Macmillan, 1968), 8.
3. John Noss, *Man's Religions,* Sixth Edition (New York: Macmillan, 1980), 336–339. Because of the importance of the Evil Spirit in Zoroaster's teaching, some scholars believe that his religion was really dualistic instead of monotheistic, that he believed in two gods of equal power, one good and the other evil. The more common opinion, however, is that Zoroaster himself believed in one Supreme Being, but that Persian priests *(Magi)* centuries after his death made the religion dualistic by stressing the power of Angra Mainyu (called *Ahriman* in later Zoroastrian writings). For more on this see James W. Boyd and Donald A. Crosby, "Is Zoroastrianism Dualistic or Monotheistic?" in *Journal of the American Academy of Religion,* 47 (1979), 557–588; Mary Boyce, *A History of Zoroastrianism* (Leiden: E. J. Brill, 1975), Volume I, 193–196.
4. R. C. Zaehner, *The Dawn and Twilight of Zoroastrianism* (New York: G. P. Putnam's, 1961), 302–321; Boyce, *History,* 233.
5. For contrasting views on the connection between Zoroastrianism and Judaism, see R. C. Zaehner, "Zoroastrianism," in *The Concise Encyclopedia of Living Faiths,* edited by R. C. Zaehner, 222; Mazani, *Zoroastrianism,* 18–25; James H. Moulton, *Early Zoroastrianism: The Origins, the Prophet, the Magi* (Amsterdam: Philo Press, 1872), 288–291, 300–301, 321–322; Boyce, *History,* 246.
6. Zaehner, *Dawn and Twilight of Zoroastrianism,* 308–311.
7. See the hymns, or Gathas (Yasna 45 and Yasna 53), quoted in Moulton, *Early Zoroastrianism,* 371, 389–390.
8. Gore Vidal, *Creation* (New York: Ballantine Books, 1982), 276–277.

9. John Blofeld, *The Tantric Mysticism of Tibet* (New York: E. P. Dutton, 1970), 58–59.
10. Kenneth K. S. Ch'en, *Buddhism: The Light of Asia* (Woodbury, NY: Barrons Educational Series, 1968), 42.

Further Reading

HESSE, HERMANN. *Siddhartha* (New York: Bantam Books, 1971). A fictionalized biography of the Buddha which captures the spirit of his message in a form attractive to twentieth-century Westerners.

VIDAL, GORE. *Creation* (New York: Ballantine Books, 1982). Well-written, if lengthy, historical novel, starring Zoroaster's grandson, which discusses the great ideas of the creative sixth century before Christ.

WATTS, ALAN. *The Way of Zen* (New York: Pantheon Books, 1957). A clear, short, and provocative interpretation of Buddhist ideas for Westerners.

ZAEHNER, R. C. *The Teachings of the Magi: A Compendium of Zoroastrian Beliefs* (New York: Oxford University Press, 1976). After the various encyclopedias, Zaehner's works are the best on this subject.

CHAPTER 3

Mahavira and Diogenes: Unconventional Men

Can a person challenge the behavior and values of the people of his society and still remain a part of that society? (Or when is a misfit not really a misfit?) Why did self-reliance and individualism take different forms in Eastern and Western societies?

We have all known people who did not seem to fit into the world in which they lived, who said "inappropriate" things, acted "funny," and generally challenged our ideas of what was socially proper. While we often write off such people as "misfits," we also often admire the social rebels—for such people can say or do things we are unable or afraid to say or do. They can provoke us to challenge our own beliefs and standards, and can lead us deeper within ourselves.

Two such unconventional individuals, whose lives posed a creative challenge to their respective societies, were Mahavira (ca. 540–468 BC), the founder of the Jain religion in India, and Diogenes of Sinope (ca. 412–323 BC), an early Cynic philosopher who lived in the Greek world of Plato and Alexander the Great. Both men challenged their society in a dramatic fashion—by personally scorning its dominant values. Both withdrew into a life of simplicity and physical hardship, but neither was able to detach himself completely from the society whose materialism and stupidities he rejected. Mahavira wandered homeless throughout India as a begging monk for thirty years, trying to free his soul from all attachments to the world. Yet he managed to establish an order of monks that grew into a full-fledged religion which has survived to our day. Diogenes was also homeless, an inhabitant of the cities of Athens and Corinth who used an old pottery jar or water cask for shelter in bad weather. Yet he did not leave the city or its people, preferring to remain a "thorn in their side," shouting insults to passersby and puncturing the pretensions of the wealthy and powerful with witty remarks that are the stuff of legend. Both individualists left the mainstream of life but kept their small boats moored close enough to the channel to make travelers uncomfortably aware they were being watched.

Like other ancient leaders who became spiritual achievers, Mahavira (the name is really a title meaning "great hero"; his given name was Vardhamma) was the son of noble parents. His father was a minor ruler in the region of Mogadsh in north India when Mahavira was born. Although Jain traditions place his birth in the year 599, many scholars believe the year 540 is more accurate. There is no doubt, however, that this sensitive young man was a product of the intellectually creative sixth and fifth centuries, the period of Buddha and Confucius in the East and of Plato in the West. Little is known of Mahavira's childhood, except that he had an older brother. One legend tells of how the young Vardhamma subdued a terrifying snake by his "courage and peaceful aura." Beyond this, "we know virtually nothing."[1]

Mahavira's spiritual development followed a pattern similar to that of other major religious leaders such as Zoroaster and Buddha. At age thirty he left his wife and child in order to seek truth by following the life of a wandering hermit. After following this life for twelve years, Mahavira had a spiritual awakening or enlightenment and became a *kevalin* (perfected soul) or a *jina* (conqueror— from which the name of the religion, Jainism, is taken). For the next thirty years, he traveled about India, organizing his disciples into an order of monks, preaching to them and to his "lay" followers, practicing severe asceticism, and following the principle of *ahimsa*—nonviolence to all living things. It was taking these two practices of asceticism and *ahimsa* to the extreme that made Mahavira an unconventional man. While traditional Hinduism had long admired the holy man who retreated to the forest, fasted, and meditated on the nature of ultimate truth as a way to attain salvation, no one before or since Mahavira pushed the principle of self-denial as far as he and his disciples did. Mahavira renounced those things we would expect a holy man to renounce (killing, lying, greed, sexual pleasure, and property) and much more. An early Jain scripture reports that when Mahavira's robe fell into shreds after a year of walking, he simply went naked—at least during the dry season. He also refused to use cold water, clean his teeth, brush vermin from his body, or scratch himself (for fear of killing living things). When people, alarmed by his appearance and behavior, abused him verbally and beat him with sticks, he refused medical treatment, "humbled himself and bore pain, free from desire." When Mahavira did take shelter, he seldom stayed in the same place more than one night, and he spent many nights sleeping in cemeteries, gardens, or in abandoned buildings.[2]

All this physical self-punishment seems neurotic to us and was even rejected by Mahavira's contemporary the Buddha, who preached a "middle way" between a life of pleasure and one of severe self-denial; yet it made sense to this man who believed that *any* attachment whatsoever to worldly things would hinder one's salvation. For Mahavira, this asceticism or self-denial was intimately related to the equally severe practice of *ahimsa*, which forbade *any* violence to *any* living thing. *Ahimsa* led Mahavira to sweep the ground before him with a small broom so that he would not accidentally step on any small creatures. He also instructed his early followers to place a cloth in front of their faces when they spoke in order to prevent "tiny forms of life" from accidentally entering the nose and mouth and being injured. Jain monks would also not eat at night since preparing food by lamplight would attract insects who would be harmed.[3]

Practicing *ahimsa* also helped the Jain monk avoid evil by avoiding attachment to material things. Like other Indians, Mahavira believed that evil deeds resulted in evil spiritual consequences (bad karma) which could keep one's soul imprisoned in the material body for many lifetimes. Mahavira interpreted this dogma, as he did the principle of *ahimsa*, very literally. He told his followers that the evil they did and the attachments they pursued would turn into bad karma which would literally "cling to the soul" and weigh it down so that it could not float free of their body when they died. One could burn off this spiritual cholesterol in somewhat the same way we get rid of its physical counterpart [fatty substances in the blood]—by fasting. It was reported that Mahavira would go months without drinking and ate very sparingly: "Sometimes he ate only the sixth meal, or the eighth, the tenth, the twelfth; without desires, persevering in meditation."[4] Mahavira pursued his principles to their logical conclusion, dying at age seventy-two by starving himself to death.

Perhaps the most interesting thing about the teachings of Mahavira is their emphasis on self-reliance. He rejected the idea that a noble birth, a high place in society, or even the favor of a god could help a person find happiness or salvation. Even prayer was pointless, and Mahavira dismissed the scriptures and rituals of Hinduism as unnecessary. Only the individual could save himself, and he could do this only by practicing extreme asceticism. Yet, despite this emphasis on the individual, Mahavira and his followers (one source reports that he had half a million by his death) did not hesitate to prescribe numerous and exacting rules for those who wished to follow the path of the Great Hero. A Jain monk started his career with a food bowl, two small water pots, a broom, a napkin, and a loincloth. Except during the rainy season, he was not allowed to stay more than three nights in one village, and even then, following the example of Mahavira, the building where he slept could not be an inhabited one. Jain monks divided the day into four periods, and they were given four duties: meditation, individual study, teaching of Jain beliefs to others, and food collection. Each of these activities was hedged with further rules and regulations. A monk could eat only thirty-two mouthfuls of food a day, for example, and each mouthful could only be the size of an egg.[5] Although all of these rules existed to promote spiritual freedom, they did this in a society in which social ties have always been important. The punishment of the body, or external asceticism, was paralleled by an "internal asceticism," an emphasis on the virtues of submission, decorum, willingness to serve, and surrender to authority.[6] By practicing these virtues, a person could free himself from the world of matter while at the same time reassuring his neighbors that his eccentricities would not disrupt their society.

Mahavira wished to become self-reliant and independent of the world without seeking to change it; after all, one could only change oneself. This was a very Indian idea, even though Mahavira pushed it further than did his Hindu or Buddhist contemporaries. Self-knowledge and self-reliance were just as important to the Greek Cynic philosopher Diogenes as they had been to Mahavira. There is even an outside chance that Diogenes may have heard of the naked Indian ascetic. In ancient times the city of Sinope on the Black Sea, where Diogenes was born, was the terminus of a trade route that brought goods from India through the Persian Gulf to Europe. Many of the beliefs and practices developed by Diogenes or attributed to him, things such as indifference to wealth, endurance of material hardship, and the importance of simplicity, were similar to those of Mahavira. For this reason one scholar has inferred that some Indian ideas were carried along the trade route from northern India to the Mediterranean world.[7] While it is certainly true that the behavior of Diogenes was as unconventional as that of Mahavira, the exact nature of the challenge he posed to his contemporaries was different— as fifth-century Greece was different from fifth-century India.

In the first place, Diogenes of Sinope was more clearly in rebellion against the values of his day than was Mahavira, who was, after all, merely taking standard Indian convictions to their logical conclusions. Almost all the stories told about Diogenes suggest that he was a wise but angry man. The word Cynic, which became the name of the philosophical school that Diogenes helped establish, came from the Greek word for dog. Diogenes was called "the dog" because of his biting wit and snappish behavior. We call a person cynical today if he or she is distrustful of human motives and has a generally low opinion of mankind. The modern word "cynic" exactly describes the behavior of Diogenes, who once tried to beg alms from a statue and when questioned by a passerby on his strange behavior, said that he was doing this in order to get practice in being refused.[8]

Perhaps we would be angry too if we were unfairly exiled from our hometown, as Diogenes may have been. Hikesias, father of Diogenes, was a prominent citizen and, for a time, the treasurer or banker of the prosperous Greek trading city of Sinope. While in this position, he systematically defaced some counterfeit coins by making gashes in them with a chisel. Although he did this in order to stabilize the city's currency, he was later accused—perhaps by political enemies—of "tampering with the coinage" and put in jail. His son and assistant, Diogenes, was exiled from Sinope; he came to Athens, in the words of one scholar, "embittered, the victim of spite and injustice . . . hating everything and everyone."[9] While this assessment of the personality of Diogenes may be too harsh, there is no doubt that this man lived a life of self-sufficiency and poverty, not in order to attain holiness or salvation but to acquire virtue *and* be a standing reproach to his fellow citizens. If Diogenes was mad, there was a method to his madness. He wanted to make his fellow Athenians and Corinthians think. He only insulted them in order to get their attention.

But insult them he did! Seeing the child of a prostitute throwing rocks into a crowd, he warned him to be careful or he'd hit his father. When he saw a bad archer practicing one day, he sat down near the target "in order not to get hit." On another occasion he asked a man who was discussing heavenly bodies with great authority: "How many days were you in coming from the sky?" This last barb shows how much Diogenes enjoyed deflating the ego of anyone—from peasant to king—who displayed self-importance. One day a bad-tempered man from whom Diogenes was begging alms offered to give the philosopher some money "if you can persuade me." "If I could have persuaded you," said Diogenes, "I would have persuaded you to hang yourself." But Diogenes was not interested in merely insulting people. He really wanted his "victims" (and other listeners) to examine their lives. In the tradition of the famous questioner Socrates, his contemporary, he used the pungent phrase and the pointed question in order to teach. A famous story about the meeting between Diogenes and the world conqueror Alexander the Great in 336 makes this point. When Diogenes did not greet the great king at the city gates of Corinth, Alexander sought out Diogenes (by now a tourist attraction in his pottery jar) and told him he could give him anything he wanted. Diogenes asked him to please stand aside since he was blocking the sunlight. It is said that Alexander remarked as he left, "If I were not Alexander, I would choose to be Diogenes."[10] Another version of their meeting contains the following exchange:

DIOGENES: "What, your majesty, is your greatest desire at present?"
ALEXANDER: "To subjugate Greece."
D: "And after you have subjugated Greece?"
A: "I will subjugate Asia Minor."
D: "And after that?"
A: "I will subjugate the world."
D: "And after that?"
A: "I plan to relax and enjoy myself."
D: "Why not save yourself all the trouble by relaxing and enjoying yourself right now?"[11]

The encounter, real or imagined, between Diogenes and Alexander emphasizes the importance of simplicity and self-examination to Diogenes. In pursuit of mastery over self, Diogenes punished his body in ways that Mahavira might have found congenial.

In addition to going nearly naked and living on the streets of Corinth in a cracked pottery jar, Diogenes practiced self-control by embracing statues in the winter and rolling his vat along the hot sand in the summer. Yet if Diogenes was an ascetic, his brand of physical self-denial was different from that of Mahavira. The Indian holy man tried to detach himself from the material world for a specific, immediate reason: Attachment to things created bad karma which kept the soul from achieving salvation. For Diogenes, bodily comforts were not necessarily evil in themselves, but they were symbols of our reliance on others. Depending upon others for our happiness was the real evil for this Greek thinker. The truly wise person required nothing that nature did not already provide. This is why Diogenes even threw away his drinking cup when he saw a young boy outdo him "in plainness of living" by drinking water from his cupped hands.[12] This is also why Diogenes made fun of the wealthy, the intellectually important (Plato, for example), or the politically powerful. Those in these categories were in danger of losing their personal, interior freedom, something that would happen if they were to rely on the goodwill, money, or praise of others.

This almost excessive self-reliance made Diogenes one of the Western world's first great individualists. But his individualism was also different from that of the great Indian teachers Mahavira and Buddha. They chose to withdraw; he chose to confront; they chose personal "religious" salvation; he chose personal ethical autonomy. The present was more important to the Greeks than the afterlife. Diogenes's ideal of independence had little to do with karma; it was more secular but also stopped short of our modern ideals of personal political rights or independence. This last point is illustrated by the story of how Diogenes got from Athens to Corinth. After residing in Athens for a number of years, the philosopher was captured by pirates while on a voyage to Aegina and taken to Crete to be sold as a slave. When asked what he was proficient in, he answered:

> "In ruling men." He then looked over the crowd gathered for the slave auction, spotted a wealthy-looking fellow, and said: "Sell me to this man; he needs a master."[13]

The wealthy Corinthian, a man named Xeniades, bought Diogenes and took him home, where the philosopher spent the last years of his life tutoring the sons of his master. Diogenes did not mind being a slave because external freedom, like today's highly regarded "financial independence," meant little to him. The most important freedom to Diogenes was the freedom to make his own moral decisions. His poverty and unconventional lifestyle helped him preserve this freedom.

Emphasis on freedom does not itself explain the general surliness and sarcasm of this famous Cynic. Diogenes once said that the most beautiful thing in the world was freedom of speech; he used this freedom to insult and provoke. A modern clinical psychologist would probably tell us that this man's insults were, in part at least, displaced resentment at his treatment by the citizens of Sinope. Diogenes also may have enjoyed the attention that his sharp tongue and eccentric life brought him. While these things may be true, it is also likely that, in addition, the barbs and witticisms for which he was famous were an integral part of his message. When he said, for example, that gold was pale because so many people were plotting against it, or when he called an ignorant rich man "the sheep with the golden fleece," this got people's attention and gave them something worth remembering and repeating—an important consideration in an age when most people could not read or write. His jeers and jokes had another purpose as well. In suggesting that the study of music, geometry, and astronomy was unnecessary, in advocating sharing of wives ("recognizing no other marriage than the union of the man who persuades with the woman who consents"), and in saying that the wine he enjoyed most was someone else's, Diogenes was not merely trying to shock people.[14] He was telling his contemporaries that everything—intellectual skills, property, even other people—could be taken lightly because they were less than ultimate, especially to the person who sought self-reliance and moral independence.

It is clear that Diogenes found it important both to live in a particular way and to make sure that his fellow citizens knew why he was living the way he was. He felt called to awaken others to the noble life of simple self-sufficiency as he had come to appreciate that life. Mahavira had earlier felt that same urge to share his good news with others, and his order of monks and the religion he began testifies to that fact. This missionary impulse on the part of both of these famous individualists is the first reason we have to think twice before calling them misfits. We might also note that true misfits would not have been remembered. It is only because the lives and words of these men challenged the people of their day that they became part of the historical record. A genuine neurotic would not reflect social values as clearly as these men did.

Mahavira and Diogenes were lucky in that each lived in a society which accepted unusual behavior. The wandering *sadhu*, or holy man, had been a part of Hindu tradition for centuries before Mahavira began his career. The pointed comments of Diogenes probably did not bother Athenians excessively because this was the city, after all, where Westerners first began to ask critical questions about nature, both human and physical. The fact that Mahavira and Diogenes were both unconventional men did not make them men without a culture. The self-reliance preached by Mahavira was a distinctly Indian product, nurtured by the holy books and Hindu practices of that subcontinent. He fertilized a spiritual plant that already existed. The less gentle type of self-reliance preached by Diogenes was as much a Greek product as *ahimsa* was an Indian one. In his own brash way, Diogenes the Cynic confirmed and advanced the skeptical, questioning spirit of classical Greece. However strange his life, his notions of moral self-sufficiency could not ultimately disturb a society that had made man (not the gods) "the measure of all things."

To be unconventional is not necessarily to exist in isolation from the values of your time and place. It can be unconventional to call men and women to live by those values they profess but ignore. It can be unconventional to take the truth quite literally, as both Mahavira and Diogenes did. If rich persons are owned by possessions, then they should dispose of such possessions. If living according to nature is a good thing, then do it—even if it means going naked or living in an old pottery jar. If a person is ennobled by suffering, then one should punish the body, not just a little for show but as much as possible. These were some of the things that this Hindu ascetic and Greek gadfly said that made them unconventional—but memorable.

One story about the death of Diogenes tells us that the eighty-nine-year-old philosopher died in a Corinth gymnasium by voluntarily holding his breath. He had supposedly left instructions that his body be thrown into a ditch and covered with a little dirt.[15] Diogenes may not have died this way, just as Mahavira may not have died by voluntarily starving himself to death. The fact that these stories, whether true or not, are told and believed is itself a tribute to the sincerity and similarity of these two men who thought and acted "otherwise."

Notes

1. Padmanabh S. Jaina, *The Jaina Path of Purification* (Berkeley: University of California Press, 1979), 6–11.
2. Akaranga-sutra, part I, in *Sacred Books of the East* (Oxford: Oxford University Press, 1884), 85–87; see also Bimala Churn Law, *Mahavira: His Life and Teaching* (London: Luzac and Co., 1937), 21–23.
3. Walter Schubring, *The Religion of the Jainas*, trans. by Anmulyachandra Sen and T. C. Burke (Calcutta: Sanskrit College, 1966), 27; *Sacred Books of the Jains*, Volume IV, *Purusartha Siddhupaya*, by Amrit Chandra Acharya (Lucknow, India: Central Jaina Publishing House, 1933), 43–44.
4. Jaina, *Jaina Path of Purification*, 113; Akaranga-sutra, part I, in *Sacred Books of the East*, 87.
5. Denise Carmody and John Carmody, *Eastern Ways to the Center: An Introduction to the Religions of Asia*. Second Edition (Belmont, CA: Wadsworth Publishing Co., 1992), 25–26; Schubring, *Religion of the Jainas*, 27–28; Louis Renou, *Religions of Ancient India* (New York: Schocken Books, 1968), 126–127.
6. Schubring, *Religion of the Jainas*, 30–31.
7. Ferrand Sayre, *Diogenes of Sinope: A Study of Greek Cynicism* (Baltimore: J. H. Furst, 1938), 39–45.
8. *Ibid.*, 7. This story, like many others about Diogenes, comes from the accounts of Diogenes Laertius (no relation), a third-century (AD) compiler of information about famous philosophers. See Diogenes Laertius, "Diogenes," in *Lives of Eminent Philosophers*, trans. by R. D. Hicks (Cambridge, MA: Harvard University Press, 1925), Volume II, 23–84. It is impossible to verify many of the anecdotes and tales told of Diogenes; some are legends or parables created later to illustrate the teachings of later Cynic philosophers. The stories do present a consistent view of Diogenes, however, and they also show that later thinkers found value in his unconventional life and thought.
9. Charles Seltman, "Diogenes: The Original Cynic," in *History Today*, Volume VI, Number 2 (February 1956), 110–115.
10. Diogenes Laertius, *Lives of Eminent Philosophers*, 63, 69, 41, 61; Plutarch, *Eight Great Lives*, edited by C. A. Robinson, Jr. (New York: Holt, Rinehart, and Winston, 1960), 76.
11. "Diogenes," in *Biographical Encyclopedia of Philosophy* (Garden City, NY: Doubleday and Company, 1965), 76.
12. Diogenes Laertius, *Lives of Eminent Philosophers*, 39.

13. *Ibid.*, 77.
14. *Ibid.*, 53, 49, 73, 75, 57.
15. *Ibid.*, 79–81.

Further Reading

LAERTIUS, DIOGENES. *Lives of Eminent Philosophers*, trans. by R. D. Hicks (Cambridge, MA: Harvard University Press, 1925), Volume II, 23–84. Best source for anecdotes about Diogenes.

LAW, BIMALA CHURN. *Mahavira: His Life and Teaching* (London: Luzac and Co., 1937). One of the few readable accounts of Mahavira in English. Also see essays in encyclopedias and textbooks on world religions.

SELTMAN, CHARLES. "Diogenes: The Original Cynic," in *History Today* (February 1956), 110–115. Very readable.

CHAPTER 4

Asoka and Shi Huangdi: Honey and Vinegar

Is it better to govern people by moral persuasion or by coercion, the carrot or the stick?

We have all heard it said that honey catches more flies than vinegar. If instead of trying to catch flies, you are trying to govern a large kingdom, the question of whether to use force or gentleness, harsh laws or ethical persuasion, can be an important one.

The Buddhist emperor of India, Asoka Maurya (291–232 BC) inherited a large, diverse kingdom and attempted—with some success—to use a "law of piety" to hold it together. Asoka's Chinese contemporary Shi Huangdi (259–210 BC), on the other hand, created a Chinese empire by consciously rejecting the moral standards for rulers prevalent in his day; he adopted the harsh practice of destroying all his enemies before they had a chance to destroy him. Both men were hard-working and self-confident. Asoka's empire crumbled within fifty years of his death, but he was remembered fondly by historians, especially Buddhist ones. Shi Huangdi, reviled by later Confucian historians, laid the foundations of an empire that lasted under various dynasties for over 2000 years. A look at the respective careers of these men will allow us to evaluate two different methods of government and the different Asian societies that made each man's style of rule not only possible but maybe even sensible.

Asoka's empire was centered in that part of northeastern India known as Magadha, but his power spread from Kabul in the northwest as far east as modern Bangladesh and as far south as the city of Madras. This Mauryan empire provided the Indian subcontinent with greater political unity than it was to have until modern times. It was founded by Asoka's grandfather Chandragupta (ruled

322–299 BC), aided by his hard-nosed political advisor Kautilya. Although Asoka came to the throne in 273 BC after the death of his father Bindusara, he was not formally crowned until 269. It took him that long to seize full power from his brothers. Buddhist sources claim he killed between six and ninety-nine of them, the larger number doubtless an exaggeration.

The cultural, social, and economic vitality and diversity of third-century India, when combined with the strong central government provided by the Mauryan rulers, made India one of very few strong civilizations at that time. In the West only the empires of Cyrus the Great and Alexander the Great rivaled it.

Cultural diversity in India was aided by the relatively "new" religions of Buddhism and Jainism. Both rejected the strict Hindu caste system which placed humans into four principal groups: priests, warriors, tradesmen and merchants, and laborers. These religions also rejected the ritual rules and the power of the Brahmins, or Hindu priests. As noted in an earlier chapter, the Buddha (560–480 BC) accepted Hindu ideas of moral cause and effect *(karma)* and of rebirth but simplified Hinduism by arguing that suffering and pain were caused by desire which itself was caused by ignorance of spiritual truth. The Buddha's Noble Eightfold Path (right or correct views, aspirations, speech, conduct, livelihood, effort, mindfulness, and meditation) would lead the believer beyond suffering to Enlightenment, or salvation. This was the Buddhist path of duty or piety *(dharma)*. Members of the Jain faith followed the teachings of another sixth-century reformer, the Mahavira (540–468 BC). Jains preached a stricter doctrine of nonviolence to all living things than did Buddhists. They also believed that salvation could be achieved by a life of strict self-denial that would free the soul from all attachment to the physical world. After his conversion to Buddhism about ten years after his coronation, Asoka's edicts preaching dharma to his people showed the influence of all three major Indian religious traditions.

Social and economic diversity in the Indian subcontinent in Asoka's day was caused not only by the racial and linguistic variety that we still see in India but also by the system of castes and subcastes that existed throughout the empire. Because the caste system was an essential part of Hinduism, as the population grew, members of the caste of merchants and traders were subdivided into hundreds of subcategories, based upon place of residence, occupation, or family membership. People were not allowed to marry out-side their caste. In short, there was a place for everyone and every-one was expected to stay in his or her place. After all, the reward for a good and stable life would be rebirth into a higher caste. This traditional Brahmanic teaching was being challenged in this period by Buddhist and Jain teachers but also by the growing economic and political powers of the merchants. Mauryan businessmen trad-ed extensively with both the Greek West and within the large em-pire. There was a thriving money economy, and merchant guilds often assumed political responsibilities. They raised groups of sol-diers for self-protection, built public buildings, controlled wages and prices, and were received at court. Merchants brought taxes and wealth to the empire and were strongly supported by the Mau-ryan rulers.

This then was Asoka's world, the one to which he addressed his famous short sermons on morality and "piety." Those of Asoka's famous "edicts" which remain are described by the surface on which they were carved: Some fourteen Rock Edicts were carved on rocks along roadways, at least ten Pillar Edicts were "written" on tall pillars in population centers, and a few Cave Edicts were in-scribed on the walls of caves, primarily for the inspiration of Bud-dhist monks. In an age without libraries or electronic mass media, this was an effective way to communicate. Tradition tells us that the king, referred to in the edicts as "Beloved of the Gods," was con-verted to Buddhism after a particularly bloody battle against the Kalinga people in the southeastern part of his empire. In this battle, fought in 262 BC, about 100,000 were slain and at least that many deported. While Asoka was a follower of Buddhism before the Kalinga war, this conflict did seem to inspire a change of heart in the king. From this time until his death, Asoka actively preached dharma to his people through edicts and tours throughout his lands; he never again engaged in a major military campaign.

But before we consign this active monarch to the realm of pious legend as a remorseful but royal monk (as many Buddhist sources do) or write him off as a cynic who used religion, we need to look more closely at the nature of his dharma. The word "dharma" is difficult to translate and the concept difficult to understand. Words such as "piety," "duty," or "morality," often used to translate "dhar-ma," suggest to many of us a fixed code of beliefs or practices for which an individual can be made strictly accountable. The Sanskrit word "dharma" refers to the duties demanded by one's station in life. While these vary for each caste, dharma requires all persons to treat others, especially family, with love and respect, to avoid those things which all men and women generally regard as evil, such as anger, cruelty, envy, pride, and the like, and to seek out that which is good: love, truth, and beauty. It is important to understand that Asoka's concept of dharma was not specifically Hindu, Buddhist, or Jain. For a Hindu, especially one in the priestly caste, following dharma would require the performance of certain rituals; for many Buddhists it involved certain monastic obligations. Beyond encouraging general ethical behavior (the king "desires security, self-control, impartiality, and cheerfulness for all living creatures"), Asoka's injunctions to his people were vague and ecumenical, showing the influence of all major Indian traditions. "Dharma is good," he wrote in Pillar Edict II, "but what does Dharma consist of? It consists of a few sins and many good deeds, of kindness, liberality, truthfulness, and purity." Who could argue with the wisdom of this? These words might help a Hindu be a better Hindu or a Buddhist be a more devout follower of the Noble Eightfold Path. And that, in the words of Rock Edict XII, is what the king wanted: "the promotion of each man's particular faith and the glorification of Dharma."[1]

King Asoka wished his subjects to be moral, but he allowed each to define the details of his or her own morality. After the midpoint of his reign, he did seem to believe genuinely that "all men are my children" and as such are capable of being trained and persuaded to live a good life. This required hard work, and Asoka set an example. He was a "morning person," rising early and engaging in prayers and meetings with the household staff before dealing with broader financial and military affairs. Breakfast at nine was followed by meetings with his council of ministers and reports from his agents. Some agents were dharma-mahamatas, or "morality ministers," who worked to see that the poor were not mistreated and that the affairs of the various religious communities were handled correctly. Asoka also built "rest stops" for weary travelers, dug wells, and kept roads in repair.

But if Asoka wished his people to be moral and reasonably comfortable, he also wanted them to continue paying taxes. He may have been a missionary, but he was not naive. In one edict, the "Beloved of the Gods" invited even those "forest people" in the remote sections of his domains "to adopt this way of life and this ideal." He reminded them, however, "that he exercises the power to punish, despite his repentance, in order to induce them to desist from their crimes."[2] Asoka's Buddhist and Jain-inspired dislike of violence never resulted in a lifting of the death penalty. His attempt to create a "national" or "imperial" morality, while a product of genuine conviction, was also a shrewd way for the monarch to centralize imperial authority in a large, culturally diverse empire. Religious toleration can be virtuous; it can also be good politics when one's empire contains dozens of different and competing sects. Kautilya, the hard-headed political realist who had helped Chandragupta create the Mauryan empire, would have found much to commend in Asoka's policy. Even the strong Buddhist flavor of Asoka's dharma was attractive to the commercial classes, who desired a moral alternative to Hindu caste restrictions. Asoka's emphasis on nonviolence appealed to the Jains, while his acceptance (though not necessarily encouragement) of caste practices avoided giving offense to the Hindus. In promoting this broad but still very Indian ethical code, Asoka, in the words of one scholar, "was attempting to reform the narrow attitude of religious teaching to protect the weak against the strong, and to promote throughout the empire a consciousness of social behavior so broad in its scope that no cultural group could object to it."[3]

Protecting the weak against the strong was the least of the worries of King Zheng of Qin [the dynasty is pronounced "chin" and Shi Huangdi was a title meaning First Emperor], the man who created a Chinese empire out of seven warring states in 221 BC. Despite his great achievement, King Zheng remains an awesome, controversial, and somewhat mysterious figure. A classic history of his reign by Sima Qian, who wrote at the beginning of the first century BC, describes this king of Qin as having "a waspish nose, eyes like slits, a chicken breast, and a voice like a jackal. He is merciless, with the heart of a tiger or wolf."[4] The Sovereign Emperor was clearly a man to be reckoned with. Both friend and foe found him formidable—and that was the way he liked it.

After coming to the throne of Qin in 246 at the age of thirteen, it took King Zheng twenty-five years to conquer the other six kingdoms in the Yellow River valley and to unify China. King Zheng (now Shi Huangdi, the First Emperor) ruled over the now-unified Chinese empire for only eleven years until his death in 210 BC, but his impact was so profound that some still argue about the wisdom of his policies and the nature of his contribution to Chinese history. Chinese folk tales lament the suffering caused by the building of the Great Wall and other imperial projects. It is understandable that a man strong enough to create an empire out of the feudal disorder that had plagued China for centuries might make a few enemies in the process. Yet this man can also be considered the father of his country. He laid the foundations for the later accomplishments of the Han dynasty (206 BC to 220 AD). Nonetheless, Shi Huangdi is almost universally condemned by Chinese historians. This animosity stems in part from the fact that they were Confucians and he was not. That he executed 460 Confucian scholars and sent others into exile after ordering all their texts burned may have also contributed to their dislike.

The roots of this conflict go back several centuries and require some understanding of Confucian philosophy. Confucius (551–479 BC), a great master of ethical philosophy, emphasized a moral code based on *li* (propriety) and *jen* (humanity). By observing proper rituals and showing respect for parents and ancestors, one demonstrated self-control and self-respect. Confucius believed in authority but he stressed the importance of virtuous behavior on the part of the ruler. If a leader practiced charity and good faith in dealing with his subjects, his kingdom would be well-governed. If all officials from the ruler to the local magistrate acted in accordance with the virtues of *li* and *jen,* the result would be order and obedience in the land. A later thinker, Mo Tzu (479–381 BC), went even further and argued that rulers should feed and clothe their people, avoid war altogether, and trust in the natural goodness of men to follow "the path of righteousness."

Education, especially one which stressed the values of the past and loyalty to the family, was important to these men. Scholarship was a path to virtue. Though this view of politics and morality would have been congenial to Asoka, it was alien to the rulers of the state of Qin, a "barbarian" frontier land. Barbarian or not, however, the rulers of Qin during the fourth century were quicker than their more civilized Chinese neighbors to end feudalism and create a strong central government, backed by a system of taxation and a powerful army. Without the family and feudal outbursts that kept other states in a condition of near-constant civil war, the Qin rulers were able to defeat the armies of the states of Han, Zhao, Wei, Yan, and Qi during the late fourth and early third centuries. By the time King Zheng became leader of Qin in 246 BC, his state was already the most powerful in the Yellow River valley. It had not reached this point by following Confucian virtues of moderation and kindness, but by following the teachings of the very different philosophy of Legalism.

The Legalists, following the ideas advanced by Han Feizi, were represented at the Qin court by Li Si, chief advisor to King Zheng and a guiding force behind many of his policies. They believed that harsh laws, speedily enforced, were more useful than moral example in securing obedience from subjects. They also suggested that troops were more effective than tedious Confucian rituals and etiquette. "Talent and wisdom," wrote Han Feizi, "are not sufficient to subdue the masses, but power and position are able to subject even men of talent." Legalists advocated what we would today call a strong, secular, amoral state. You can win by doing those things that your enemies would be ashamed to do, one Legalist text advised. Legalist philosophy and Qin ambition were made for each other. Li Si got a job and a chance to be a powerful man. The Qin ruler found someone who would tell him that killing several hundred soldiers after they surrendered was not really all that bad. Li Si advised his king to bribe the feudal lords of other states; "as for those who were unwilling, they were to be stabbed with sharp swords" and the army sent to finish the job.[5]

Despite (or perhaps because of) his Legalist disdain for morality, Shi Huangdi's specific and lasting achievements were impressive. He turned China from a patchwork of squabbling kingdoms into a state governed from a central capital at Xianyang. When King Zheng conquered a state, he sent the ruling family and others who might challenge his power to his capital—and sold their land. He also organized his realm into provinces and prefectures or counties. The former were originally military districts while the latter were administrative ones and used for purposes of tax collection. Eventually civil and military leaders were placed in each province. Since these officials were not members of the emperor's family or of high noble rank (as they might have been under the old system), there was less chance they would try to challenge the emperor. Besides, placing a number of major officials in each of his thirty-six provinces almost guaranteed that they would quarrel with each other; this left final authority in the hands of the emperor.

Shi Huangdi's efforts to centralize took other forms as well. He standardized weights and measures, the characters used to write the Chinese language (to allow officials to communicate with those who spoke dialects), and even the length of cart axles so that all carts could use the same ruts or tracks. The First Emperor also created the first civil service and paid officials in coin, not in land, out of the taxes they helped collect. There were no private armies during Shi Huangdi's reign, and the laws of the land were public, if very harsh. Finally, the new emperor built many roads, several hundred new palaces, and elaborate defensive fortifications in the north known as the Great Wall.

Shi Huangdi's building projects, however, illustrate his extravagance. His Great Wall, which connected and strengthened existing fortifications, was needed to protect China from the nomadic tribes of Turks and Mongols who periodically attacked and devastated Chinese cities. Whether China needed a wall 1400 miles long, with thousands of watchtowers, is debatable. The nearly one million men who labored and died building it over twelve years would probably disagree. Nearly as many men, 700,000, spent thirty years building an elaborate tomb for the emperor at Mount Li, near Xi'an and the Yellow River. Part of the tomb consisted of a three-acre flat-roofed underground vault containing life-sized, individualized statues of an army of 8000 men and horses, including full-scale bronze chariots and charioteers, and images of all members of the emperor's family and household staff. While Shi Huangdi was not the first to construct an elaborate grave site (earlier Shang dynasty rulers buried real people instead of statues), the magnitude of Shi Huangdi's effort helps us understand why some called him a megalomaniac.[6]

He also built 270 palaces near his capital, some of them replicas of those of his conquered enemies. These were justified for security reasons since they allowed him to sleep in a different place every night. One precise and telling example of the emperor's arrogance is found in Sima Qian's history. On one occasion a "great gale" prevented the ruler's ship from crossing the Yangtze River near the temple of Mount Xiang. In order to punish the local goddess, the Princess of the River Xiang, "the emperor in his rage made 3000 convicts cut down all the trees on Mount Xiang, leaving the mountain bare."[7] Clearly, this man took himself very seriously. He believed himself to be the first of a line of 10,000 emperors. Shi

Huangdi's inscriptions did not urge men to live morally; they bragged that "his influence knows no end, his will is obeyed and his orders will remain through eternity."[8]

Of course, Shi Huangdi's enemies and their ideas did outlive him. By the end of the Qin dynasty in 206 BC, the philosophy of Legalism was thoroughly discredited by the excesses of Shi Huangdi and his son. Both Han Feizi and Li Si died violent deaths. It was fitting that the first of the rebellions that broke out after Shi Huangdi's death was led by two farmers who were late in reporting for forced labor on one of the imperial projects. Since the penalty for being late was immediate execution, they decided their chances of survival would be better if they started a revolt. It was the first of many that led to the collapse of the Qin empire. Had the law been less stringent, this revolt may not have started.

This point was quickly made by Confucian historians, beginning with the famous essay on "The Faults of Qin," written by the Han dynasty poet and statesman Jia Yi (201–169 BC). He remarked on the military skill of Qin generals but then asked why such a feared dynasty could be overthrown with such relative ease. Jia's answer has echoed through twenty centuries of Chinese history: "Because it failed to rule with humanity and righteousness and to realize that the power to attack and the power to retain what one has won are not the same."[9] The general verdict was that Shi Huangdi and his dynasty got what they deserved. We might note in passing that perhaps the Confucian historians were a bit insincere and self-righteous, since none of them regretted Chinese unification but only the methods that had been used to achieve it.

Perhaps the moral of this story, if there is one, is that both honey and vinegar are necessary. One historian of China has written that although "force can never give a permanent unity. . . . its use may be necessary to establish this unity in the beginning." The accomplishments of the Han period would have been impossible without the achievements of the preceding Qin empire.[10] The Buddhist Asoka was both realistic and pious. He received better treatment from historians than did Shi Huangdi, but his empire survived him by only a few decades. At least Asoka did understand that force had its place but that some things simply cannot be forced. In one of his edicts he noted that "people can be induced to advance in dharma by only two means, by moral prescriptions and by meditation." He confessed that morals were "of little conse-

quence but meditation was of great importance. . . . it is by meditation that people have progressed in Dharma most."[11]

Notes

1. *The Edicts of Asoka*, edited and trans. by N. A. Nikam and Richard McKeon (Chicago: University of Chicago Press, 1959), 41, 52.
2. *Ibid.*, 28–29.
3. Romila Thapar, *Asoka and the Decline of the Mauryas* (Oxford: Oxford University Press, 1961), 181.
4. Li Yu-ning, editor, *The First Emperor of China* (White Plains, NY: International Arts and Sciences Press, 1975), 264.
5. Derk Bodde, *China's First Unifier: A Study of the Ch'in Dynasty as Seen in the Life of Li Si, 280–208 BC* (Hong Kong: Hong Kong University Press, 1967), 189, 14–15. [The name of the Qin dynasty and state is spelled Ch'in in all but the most recently published works.]
6. Audrey Topping, "China's Incredible Find," *National Geographic* (April 1978), 440–459; Audrey Topping, "Clay Soldiers: The Army of Emperor Chin," *Horizon* (January 1977), 2, 4–13.
7. Li Yu-ning, editor, *The First Emperor of China*, 275.
8. *Ibid.*, 271–272.
9. *Ibid.*, 281–282.
10. Bodde, *China's First Unifier*, 236–237.
11. *Edicts of Asoka*, 40.

Further Reading

Edicts of Asoka. Edited and trans. by N. A. Nikam and Richard McKeon (Chicago: University of Chicago Press, 1959). Sample Asoka's ideas directly.

GOKHALE, B. K. *Asoka Maurya* (New York: Twayne Publishers, 1966). Best short biography of Asoka.

TOPPING, AUDREY. "China's Incredible Find," *National Geographic Magazine* (April 1978), 440–459. The title is not an exaggeration; see for yourself.

WALEY, ARTHUR. *Three Ways of Thought in Ancient China* (London: Allen and Unwin, 1931). See the chapter on "The Realists" for a good description of Legalism.

CHAPTER 5

Constantine and Julian: How the Galileans Won

To what extent can the spread of a religion be promoted or restricted by the personality or decisions of a ruler?

Some things have been around so long that it is hard to imagine the world without them. One of those is the Christian religion. Although not as old as Hinduism, Buddhism, or Judaism, Christianity has been such a formative influence in Western history that we make the birth of Christ a focal point in history by dating time as either BC (Before Christ) or AD (Anno Domini—the year of the Lord).

We hardly notice this bias because most of us grew up in a culture where Judeo-Christian values defined what was normal. For centuries in the West, we have understood religion in terms of rabbis and priests, churches and covenants, God and grace, and heaven and hell. It was not always this way. As late as three hundred years after the birth of Christ, it was not yet clear that Christianity would become the religion of the Roman world; it was certainly not clear that this new religion would dominate the new Germanic kingdoms that were to succeed the Roman empire in the western part of Europe. The actions of two fourth-century emperors, Constantine (280–337 AD) and Julian (330–363 AD), can help us understand how Christianity spread from a minority sect within the Roman empire to become a major political and religious force within less than a century.

Constantine was the more revolutionary of these men, but Julian was the more intriguing. Constantine became ruler in 306, offered "complete toleration" to Christians (about ten percent of his subjects) from 313, and spent many of the next twenty-five years trying to ensure the welfare of his empire by supporting the Christian God; he was baptized only on his deathbed. Julian, known in Christian history as Julian the Apostate [meaning someone who had the faith but abandoned it], was born a Christian but converted to paganism. During his short reign as sole emperor from 361 to 363 he attempted to restore paganism to favor in the Roman empire. His attempt to reverse Constantine's work was doomed, whether by circumstances or by his "noble but erratic character"[1] we can never be sure. His failure has intrigued modern historians and novelists, some of whom consider him a tragic hero and others a fool.

In order to understand both the success of Christianity in fourth-century Rome and the actions of these two men, we must appreciate the fears and problems of fourth-century citizens of the Roman empire. It was a time of political and economic crisis. The Romans, by the end of the third century, were short of both manpower (for farms and armies) and money. Unfortunately, they had plenty of "barbarians," Germanic tribesmen east of the Rhine and north of the Danube rivers who wished to enter the empire. In addition, there was no systematic way for emperors to be replaced; on the death of one ruler, it was often the general with the strongest army who became the next one. The Emperor Diocletian (ruled 284–305) attempted to remedy some of these problems by dividing the empire into east and west (with the Balkan states the approximate dividing line), placing an emperor, or Augustus, and an "assistant emperor," or Caesar, in each half. When the Augustus died or resigned, the Caesar was supposed to become the new emperor and appoint a new Caesar. This system of government, known as the Tetrarchy [rule by four], looked good on paper but did not work. In 306 Constantine became Caesar upon his father's death not because he was appointed but because he was named a ruler by his troops. He established his position as Augustus in the west through successful civil wars. Diocletian's attempts to halt inflation and the manpower decline by fixing wages and prices and by insisting that a person not leave a job or city without permission were also well-intentioned failures. For one thing, he did not have enough troops to enforce these edicts. He did have enough, however, to launch, with his co-emperor, Galerius, the last great persecution of the Christians, from 303 to 311. The memory of this brief but bitter persecution made Constantine's decision to tolerate Christianity in 313 that much more dramatic.

While Constantine's shift of emphasis from the pagan gods to the Christian God was dramatic, his public religiosity was not. In fourth-century Rome, almost everyone was religious or, to use a later word favored by Christian writers, superstitious. The person who did not believe that demons, gods, and spirits of various sorts were active in the daily lives of all men and women was rare. The supernatural was a natural part of life at that time and foolish was the politician who would claim to "separate church and state." Indeed, one of the pagan charges against the Galileans (as Julian was to call them in order to emphasize their rural, provincial origins) was that they were "atheists" because they refused to worship the state-sponsored gods. Political and economic difficulties affected everyone in the Roman empire, especially people in the less urbanized western provinces, by the fourth century. That religion, whether pagan or Christian, should be used to help men solve political problems was clear to decision makers in this period.

These two facts of life in 300 AD—political and economic crisis and the religiosity of the Romans—allow us to understand this man Constantine in terms other than the miraculous ones in which he was described by the famous early Christian historian Eusebius. According to this bishop and friend of Constantine, the emperor, shortly before the battle of Milvian Bridge in 312, saw the monogram for the word Christ (Chi Rho—☧) written in the sky along with the words "In this sign you will conquer." Another story has Christ, in a vision, commanding Constantine to place the Christian sign on the shields of his soldiers before the battle. In any case (and historians disagree on whether the "cross in the sky" story is true in some sense or merely a fabrication by a Christian apologist) Constantine did win the battle and from that time on showed imperial favor to the Christian God. It began with the famous Edict of Milan issued with his co-emperor, Licinius, in 313:

> We have decided . . . to grant both to the Christians and to all others perfect freedom to practice the religion which each has thought best for himself, that so whatever Divinity resides in heaven may be placated, and rendered propitious [friendly] to us and to all who have been placed under one authority.

The words of this edict, which granted toleration to Christians, are interesting. The Christian God, Constantine believed, had granted him victory; it was sheer folly not to acknowledge the power of that god. The edict "publicly admits" the Christian God into the Roman state worship; for a decade after 312 Constantine saw no problem in also putting the image of the Sun God, Apollo or Sol Invictus, on his coins.[2] It was only in later years that Constantine's toleration of Christianity turned into an active, personal commitment to this religion. In the early years when the emperor's faith in the Christian message was not as strong as it would later become, it seems clear that he supported Christianity as much to promote the good of the state as out of personal conviction. For political reasons, he never outlawed pagan worship nor made Christianity the exclusive, official state religion.

All this is not to question the sincerity of Constantine's belief in Christ. It is only to explain that Constantine, like any fourth-century Roman ruler, worshipped his God, as one historian put it, "on his own terms."[3] Constantine's religious convictions were his own, but they were sincere, as he proved time and again during the last twenty-five years of his life. Shortly after the victory at Milvian Bridge, Constantine granted Christian clergy important immunities from state service and some taxes. In 321, he made all bequests to the Christian church legal and ordered all courts and work places closed on Sunday, "the venerable day of the Sun."[4] While this last decision might indicate the continuing "confusion" on Constantine's part between Christ and Apollo, these measures, taken together, were to give Christians a favored place, legally and socially, in the Roman world. And this was only the beginning. Constantine had a passion for church building and built seven churches in Rome, including the original St. Peter's, one to St. Paul, and the Church of St. John Lateran. He endowed or supported financially other churches at Naples, Ostia, and Alba in Italy, and built numerous churches in the eastern part of the empire, some of them on the sites of former pagan temples. In his new eastern capital of Constantinople, he dedicated a Church of the Apostles on the site of a former temple to the goddess Aphrodite.[5] The pagan taxpayers must have grumbled, even though the emperor did continue to appoint some pagans to high positions in his government.

Many religious leaders today recognize state support of religion as a mixed blessing since the power to support is also the power to control. Historians have even developed a term, *Caesaropapism*, to describe a situation in which the civil power or Caesar dominated the religious power or church (papism refers to the chief religious authority of the European Middle Ages, the pope). Constantine was the founder of this tradition of imperial control over ecclesiastical policy, a tradition that was never challenged in the eastern Roman, or Byzantine, empire and was only gradually challenged in the western part of Europe. The bishops of Constantine's day were undismayed when the emperor called the great church council at Nicea in the year 325. Constantine certainly thought this action appropriate; as a pagan ruler, he was *pontifex maximus*, or head of the state religion. He would have no reason to assume that his authority over his Christian subjects should be less than over his pagan ones. Besides, by this time, as one scholar recently argued, Constantine had personally become "a sincere and convinced adherent" of the Christian faith. In a sermon delivered on Good Friday in 325, just weeks before he decided to call the meeting at Nicea, the emperor showed himself to be a man genuinely persuaded of God's providence over the world and a person truly interested in defending Christianity against its pagan detractors. Constantine was the first Christian, for example, to see in the writings of earlier pagan authors (in this case, Virgil) a prefiguring of the coming of Christ.[6] To promote unity among Christians as well as to better govern the empire, Constantine wished to help his fellow Christians settle their theological differences.

The chief dispute at the Council of Nicea was over the nature of Christ. The basic Christian doctrine of the Incarnation—the belief that Christ is truly God but also truly man—strained logic. Therefore, during these early centuries various thinkers tried to simplify it by making Christ either one or the other, a God who just appeared to be a man or a man who was Godlike. At the time of Nicea, Bishop Arius of Alexandria was creating problems by saying that God was indivisible and hence Christ was less important than God the Father. At the insistence of the emperor, the bishops at Nicea agreed, some very reluctantly, to accept a creed (known in later form as the Nicene Creed) which stated that the Son was of the same essence as the Father. While that did not solve the problem immediately, it is significant that the theological formula suggested by Constantine did eventually become the creed recited today in many Christian churches.

For Constantine, the unity of the church was far more important than any particular theological formula. Extensive arguments over the purity of faith and doctrine were apparently as tedious to the emperor as they are to many Christians today. He expressed his frustration on one occasion when he told a man who preached that Christians who had denied their faith during the days of persecution could not be readmitted to the community of faith: "Set up a ladder and mount to heaven alone." On another occasion, Constantine displayed his impatience by telling an assembly of bishops that it was

> better to address ourselves to the objects within our powers and within the reach of our nature, for what persuades us in the course of a debate distracts most of us from the truth of reality, as has befallen many philosophers who exercised their wits on reasons and investigations of the essence of things.[6]

"The Supreme Divinity," as Constantine typically called Him, wished for all to worship sincerely and in peace with one another. This, as the emperor saw it, was why he had been granted the victory over his foes: in order to ensure such peace and unity. That was why he built so many churches and called church councils to bring about theological peace and harmony. After the Council of Nicea, Constantine wrote in a letter that "Divine Providence" had granted "fullness of grace that we may, freed from all error, acknowledge one and the same faith. No longer can the devil work his will against us." It was the Devil, he believed, who caused such things as street riots, bad harvests, challenges to imperial authority, and various works of witchcraft.[7] Any strong ruler would do all in his power to prevent such evils. Any ruler would also seek divine aid. The history of Western civilization was changed because the God that Constantine called upon for aid was the Christian one. That is what made this particular man a hero to Bishop Eusebius and a revolutionary historical figure.

We can better appreciate the revolutionary nature of Constantine's conversion to Christianity by contrasting his career with that of his nephew, the Emperor Julian. In trying to understand Julian, it is important to remember, especially when he is called a "fanatic," a "muddleheaded enthusiast," or "a trifle unbalanced,"[8] that his side lost—and history is written by the victors. The difficulty of forming an accurate picture of this emperor is illustrated by these contrasting views of Julian's physical appearance. His enemy, the Christian writer Gregory of Nazianzen, saw the emperor's character expressed in his "unsteady neck, twitching and hunched shoulders, wandering eye with its 'crazy' look, uncertain and swaying walk, proud and haughty nose . . . uncontrolled and hysterical laughter, halting and panting speech." A far more sympathetic pagan historian, Ammianus Marcellinus, described Julian as a man whose "eyes were fine and full of fire, an indication of the acuteness of his mind. His eyebrows were handsome, his nose very straight, his mouth somewhat large with a pendulous lower lip. His neck was thick and somewhat bent, his shoulders large and broad."[9] In assessing Julian, perhaps we could agree, if only for the sake of argument, that the pagan beliefs of this thick-necked, stoop-shouldered ruler were as sincere as the Christian beliefs of his uncle. Some historians think that the narrow-minded dogmatism of Constantine's son and successor Constantius may have turned Julian against Christianity; the murder of all members of Julian's family by this Christian emperor may have helped as well. Whatever his motives—his dislike of the hypocrisy of some Christians or his attraction to the non-Christian philosophy of some of his early teachers—by his early twenties Julian had become a secret adherent of several pagan religions.

Unaware of Julian's pagan beliefs, the Emperor Constantius made him a Caesar in 355 and sent him off to fight the Germans in Gaul. Constantius did not trust Julian, but the young man was his last living relative and perhaps Constantius felt that his execution of Julian's brother Gallus the year before would serve as a warning against sedition. Surprisingly, the intellectual Julian proved to be a competent and popular general. He was so popular that in 360 when Constantius, growing short of manpower and increasingly suspicious, sent orders to move four of Julian's best regiments to the eastern front to fight the Persians, some of his troops rebelled and forced an imperial crown upon the reluctant (to hear him say it anyway) Julian. During the remainder of that year, Julian attempted to work out an agreement with Constantius. When this proved impossible, Julian began a civil war against him in 361. In the fall of that year Constantius died, and in December Julian entered Constantinople as the new emperor, finally able to begin his campaign against the Galileans.

Julian doubtless wished the best for his subjects. Despite a half century of official support for Christianity, a majority of the inhabitants of the empire remained pagan, many of them farmers still attached to their local gods (the word "pagan" originally meant country dweller). After donning the purple emperor's robe, Julian disallowed special exemptions that Christian priests had been granted. Julian did not wish to persecute Christians actively but rather hoped, in the words of one of his biographers, to win new adherents to the traditional gods by pointing out to people "the absurdities of Christian doctrine and the duplicity and hypocrisy of Christian practice." In 362, the emperor wrote to a friend:

> I affirm by the gods that I do not wish the Galileans to be either put to death or unjustly beaten, to suffer any other injury . . . nevertheless I do assert absolutely that the god-fearing must be preferred to them. For through the folly of the Galileans almost everything has been overturned, whereas by the grace of the gods we are all preserved.[10]

Julian's most controversial religious measure was an edict of 362 denying Christians the right to teach the pagan classics in the schools. He did this because, in his own words, "when a man thinks one thing and teaches his pupils another, in my opinion he fails to educate exactly in proportion as he fails to be an honest man."[11] Since Julian believed that education was second only to military service in importance to the state, this edict made sense. Ironically, had Julian succeeded in separating Christianity from classical learning, it would have destroyed that which he loved. Without Christians to preserve classical texts, most would have been lost in the centuries after Julian.

Among moderns, Julian's image is enhanced by the fact that he was personally a most moral, even ascetic, sort of person. He lived a simple life and dismissed court officials who dressed ostentatiously; Ammianus Marcellinus noted that Julian dismissed a splendidly dressed barber with these words: "I sent for a barber, not a fiscal agent."[12] The emperor drank sparingly and did not engage in those sins of the flesh that readers of Roman history expect of pagan emperors; in fact, Julian remained celibate after the death of his wife. He preferred reading or writing to throwing parties. His bearded appearance and his lifestyle offended the citizens of Antioch during his nine months' residence before he departed on his final campaign against the Persians in 363. Julian contemptuously dismissed his Antiochene critics in a most unimperial fashion by writing a satire. His *Misopogon or Beard Hater* poked fun at himself and criticized the intolerance of his subjects who felt their ruler did not fit the imperial mold. That, perhaps as much as his religious policy, might explain the resentment against him in upper-class court circles.

Yet, however high-minded and misunderstood might have been this philosopher-emperor's attempt to save Rome by withdrawing favor from those who neglected the gods,[13] his efforts were doomed to failure. Julian died during his ill-fated campaign against the Persians in the summer of 363, a campaign undertaken against the advice of both his political advisors and his priests. He was thirty-one and had governed Rome for only twenty months. Had Julian ruled, like Constantine, for thirty years, would his campaign to revive paganism have succeeded? Could he, given time, have separated Christianity from the Roman state? If he had been able to do this, what effect would this have had on the empire, or on Christianity?

Although historians can only speculate on the answer to such intriguing questions, the answer to the first and most important question is almost certainly no. Had Julian remained the *pontifex maximus* for a generation, the upper classes might have remained pagan a bit longer. The lower classes would probably not have been much affected by Julian's preachings, both because he did not have the common touch and because his paganism appealed mainly to intellectuals. In his *Hymn to the Mother of the Gods*, he stripped a religion that had stressed the fertility of man and nature of all its sexual meaning and interpreted the story of Cybele in purely metaphysical terms. This was not something the mass of Romans could identify with—in thirty or three hundred years. Even given more time, Julian would have found it hard to separate Christianity from the Roman state. By the fourth century, the church "had become a secular as well as a spiritual phenomenon: it was a huge force for stability, with its own traditions, property, interests and hierarchy." Its interests—as an organization which was "universal, ecumenical, orderly, international, and multi-racial"—blended well with those of the international and multi-racial Roman empire.[14] By this time, the church and the empire needed each other. Also, despite the "democratic" traditions in Greece and Rome, the hierarchical principle was firmly established in the Roman world and it was strengthened rather than weakened by political crises. Whatever religion would finally dominate the Mediterranean world would doubtless have to rely on help from the state, however dangerous modern Americans might consider such reliance. Perhaps the best that Julian could have done, had he lived another thirty years, would be to sustain religious diversity into the fifth century. Even without Constantine's help, Christianity was winning in fourth-century Rome. It was an open religion, without social distinctions and with administrative careers open to talent. Christianity competed successfully with the mystery religions of Cybele, Isis, and Mithra, each of which was more limited in appeal but all of which offered a sense of community and the belief in an afterlife. In flatly opposing paganism, Christianity offered individuals a clear choice, something always psychologically welcome in an age of turmoil and uncertainty.[15] Had he lived longer, Julian might have made it necessary for Christianity to compete with pagan religions a bit longer; that could have strengthened, not weakened, the Galileans.

In the final analysis, the decisions of Constantine in the year 313 and later did mark a turning point in Roman and Western history. His actions began a tradition of Christian reliance on government that has remained, off and on, for good or ill, an important part of Christian history. Constantine was not responsible for the success of Christianity, but he did determine the *way* in which the religion of the Galilean would influence later European history. Julian was unable to wean the Romans away from this new religion, despite his sincere but impractical measures. Julian died young; it is significant that no one tried to follow in his footsteps. Perhaps later rulers understood these words of Julian better than he did: "Not to see beforehand what is possible and . . . impossible in practical affairs is a sign of the utmost foolishness."[16]

Notes

1. R. H. Schmandt, "Julian the Apostate," in *New Catholic Encyclopedia* (New York: McGraw-Hill, 1967), Volume 8, 47.
2. John B. Firth, *Constantine the Great: The Reorganization of the Empire and the Triumph of the Church* (Freeport, NY: Books for Libraries Press, 1971), 107–114; Ramsay MacMullen, *Constantine* (New York: Dial Press, 1969), 110–112.
3. MacMullen, *Constantine*, 113.
4. A. H. M. Jones, *Constantine and the Conversion of Europe* (New York: Macmillan, 1949), 91, 99–100.
5. Robert M. Grant, *Early Christianity and Society* (New York: Harper and Row, 1977), 151–154; MacMullen, *Constantine*, 154.

6. Robin Lane Fox, *Pagans and Christians* (New York: Alfred A. Knopf, 1986), 627–662.

7. MacMullen, *Constantine*, 163.

8. Norman F. Baynes, *Constantine the Great and the Christian Church*, Second Edition (Oxford: Oxford University Press, 1972), 21; MacMullen, *Constantine*, 239.

9. G. W. Bowerstock, *Julian the Apostate* (Cambridge, MA: Harvard University Press, 1978), 119; Robert Browning, *The Emperor Julian* (Berkeley: University of California Press, 1976), xi; Harold Mattingly, *Christianity in the Roman Empire* (New York: Norton, 1967), 68.

10. Browning, *Emperor Julian*, 66; John C. Rolfe, trans., *Ammianus Marcellinus* (Cambridge, MA: Harvard University Press, 1963), Volume II, 513.

11. Browning, *Emperor Julian*, 109; W. C. Wright, trans., *Works of the Emperor Julian* (Cambridge, MA: Harvard University Press, 1962), Volume III, 23.

12. Wright, *Works*, III, 117–121; see also Glanville Downey, "The Emperor Julian and the Schools," *The Classical Journal*, V (1957–1958), 97–103.

13. *Ammianus Marcellinus*, II, 201.

14. Paul Johnson, *A History of Christianity* (New York: Atheneum, 1976), 76.

15. E. R. Dodds, *Pagan and Christian in an Age of Anxiety* (New York: Norton, 1970), 133–138.

16. Wright, *Works*, III, 299.

Further Reading

CARSON, R. A. G. "Emperor Constantine and Christianity," *History Today*, Volume 6 (January 1956), 12–20.

GRANT, ROBERT M. *Early Christianity and Society* (New York: Harper and Row, 1977). Helps place these men in context; examines social role of early Christians.

MACMULLEN, RAMSAY. *Constantine* (New York: Dial Press, 1969). One of the most interesting biographies.

VIDAL, GORE. *Julian* (New York: Little, Brown, 1964). Exciting and sympathetic novel about Julian which suggests he was killed by a Christian soldier.

CHAPTER 6

Irene and Wu Zhao: Two Iconoclasts

What qualities do women rulers need in order to succeed in a society dominated by males?

The word "iconoclast" has two different but related meanings. Originally this word (literally "image breaker") referred to those Greek Christians in the eastern Roman, or Byzantine, empire during the eighth and ninth centuries who opposed the use of images in religious worship. A modern dictionary notes that an iconoclast is, more commonly, "one who attacks and seeks to overthrow traditional or popular ideas or institutions."[1]

Empress Irene, actual ruler of the Byzantine empire for much of the period between 780 and 802 AD, was most certainly not an iconoclast in the religious sense of the term; in fact, she was perhaps the most famous opponent of the eighth-century image breakers and she helped ensure their defeat. However, both Irene and her near-contemporary, the Chinese empress Wu Zhao (625–705 AD), were iconoclasts in the more modern sense of that term. In the ancient world, women were not considered qualified to rule. Although royal women in ancient Egypt occasionally exercised power, the most famous of these, Hatshepsut (reigned 1486–1468 BC), ruled as a "king" rather than a queen, illustrating the fact that it was easier for a woman "to adapt herself to fit the titles than to change the titles to fit her sex." When she died, her nephew tried to destroy all evidence that she had ruled.[2] Ruling a large state was seen as a distinctly male task, and both Wu Zhao and Irene attacked this widespread conviction. Although both followed the convention of ruling in the names of their husbands or sons, each also eventually went beyond this to rule in her own name. Both also governed their states successfully enough that even some male critics admitted their competence. Both were also accused of much intrigue, and each saw such behind-the-scenes maneuvering as the only way to secure power in a man's world.

Facts about the early years of Irene are scanty. She was born in Athens and orphaned early in life. Her piety and dazzling beauty brought her to the attention of Emperor Leo IV, who married the seventeen-year-old in 769. Beginning with the eighteenth-century English historian Edward Gibbon, who referred to Irene's "haughty spirit" and to her ambition which "stifled every sentiment of humanity and nature," historians have gone out of their way to condemn Irene's character.[3] Words like "unscrupulous," "cruel," and "diabolical" are used to describe her actions and intentions. Of her desire for power, there is little doubt; whether her use of that power was wise or not is open to interpretation.

Even had she sought power in a more traditionally feminine fashion and exercised it behind the scenes, Irene would be famous for her role in the iconoclast controversy. Her husband, a determined opponent of images, worked hard to enforce a decree of a church council of 754 which made anyone who possessed or used "the evil art of painters" in worship an enemy of both church and state. Supported by the army, court clergy, and upper classes who saw the use of images as idolatry, the emperor forced the masses to take an oath swearing they would not worship images. Most monks supported the use of paintings as proper devotion and, because of this, many monasteries were seized by the state during the mid-eighth century and turned into barracks and arsenals for the army. Women were particularly suspected of being iconophiles ("lovers of images"), and Irene herself was accused of being "lying and unscrupulous" because she presumably hid her iconophile views until the death of Leo IV in 780.

For the next ten years Irene ruled the Byzantine empire as regent for Constantine VI, her ten-year-old son. During this time, she made peace with the Muslim Arabs in 783 and sought a closer relationship in the West with the Emperor Charlemagne and the Roman papacy. Her most notable achievement, however, was to secure a decree from a church council in 787 which officially restored the use of images in churches, noting (as did the Western Roman church) that such pictures of Christ and the saints were to be "venerated" and not "adored." The monks, or "devout party," were victorious and they hailed Irene as "the Christ-supporting Empress, whose government . . . is a symbol of peace."[4]

Such praise from the monks did little to endear the empress to the iconoclastic military men, especially to those who blamed their military defeats at the hands of the Bulgars (788) and Muslims on the rule of a woman. Irene also withheld all power from her son and gave it to her favorites, especially the eunuch [castrated] Stauracius. Army opposition to Irene led to mutiny in 790, and Irene was forced to turn over the government to her son Constantine VI. This is when the real intrigue began.

Irene spent the next two years rebuilding her "power base." According to Edward Gibbon, Irene "flattered the bishops and eunuchs, revived the filial tenderness of the prince, regained his confidence, and betrayed his credulity."[5] By 792 Irene, who was once again called the Empress, was an unofficial co-ruler with Constantine. She would not be content until she secured full control of the state. Though critics accused her of plotting to bring about Constantine VI's downfall, this was not hard since Constantine assisted in weakening himself. In 792, when his uncles threatened the throne, he punished them by blinding the eldest and cutting out the tongues of the other four. Irene's critics say she "persuaded" him to do this. While she may or may not have been behind this maiming, it is certain that she encouraged Constantine's fondness for and adultery with one of her servant girls, Theodote, whom he married after divorcing his wife. When the devout monks protested this relationship, he lost patience and finally arrested, beat, and imprisoned a group of them at the Sakkudion monastery. Whatever Irene's role in all this, Constantine's behavior does not mark him as an effective ruler.

Little love was lost between mother and son during their seven years of joint rule. By the summer of 797 Irene was actively conspiring against her son. Once he became aware of this, Constantine fled the capital city of Constantinople but was soon arrested on the Asian shore of the Bosphorus. At Irene's orders, the punishment he had inflicted upon his eldest uncle was visited upon Constantine: His eyes were put out so that he could never rule again. This was the heinous crime that Gibbon believes "may not be paralleled in the history of crimes."[6] In Irene's defense, we should note that her behavior was little different from that of earlier male rulers. Besides, she could have killed Constantine outright. But that would have been murder—and much more sinful.

Despite the reproach historians heaped upon Irene, the last five years of her reign were prosperous and peaceful for her and the empire. She patronized the arts, built convents, and contributed considerable sums to charity. More importantly, by lowering taxes and import duties, she provided genuine help to her poor subjects who had been abused by tax collectors. And although Irene rode to church in a golden chariot pulled by four white horses, she scattered money among the poor as she passed through the streets of Constantinople.

Unfortunately, Irene's victory did not bring an end to either the iconoclast controversy or plots by the palace nobility and eunuchs. A combination of lingering religious resentments and palace intrigue led to her overthrow in 802. After her former finance minister Nicephorus seized the throne, she made a dignified speech and then spent her last year of life supporting herself by spinning on the island of Lesbos where she was sent in exile. She might have been comforted had she known that the iconoclasts would in the end lose their fight to ban images. When that day came, the clergy whom she had consistently supported saw to it that this proud, passionate, and ambitious woman was made a saint of the Greek Orthodox Church. She became "the most pious Irene."

Irene of Byzantium appears saintly when compared with Wu Zhao, the equally beautiful woman who moved from concubine to sole ruler of Asia's most powerful empire. Wu Zhao's Chinese empire was larger than that of Irene, her tenure of power longer, and her sins of greater enormity: For her, murders and plots were almost routine. Wu Zhao, like Irene, seized and held power by intrigue.

Born in 625, Wu Zhao was thirteen when she became a Concubine of the Fifth Grade at the court of the Emperor Taizong in 638. Her beauty and ambition gave her an advantage over the 122 concubines of various "grades" at the Tang emperor's court in Chang'an. Although imperial concubines were supposed to be strictly secluded from all but the emperor, Wu Zhao fell in love with the emperor's son and was reputedly intimate with him before Taizong died in 649. Her morally reprehensible but practical liaison with the future emperor is an example of Wu Zhao's shrewdness; it alerts us to a talent she exploited throughout her career.

Following Taizong's death his wives and concubines were sent, as was customary, to a Buddhist convent where they were expected to live out their days quietly. Within eighteen months, however, Wu Zhao was back at the palace as a concubine of the new Gaozong emperor, with whom she had been intimate several years earlier.

Ironically, Empress Wang encouraged her husband to resume his old relationships in the hope that Wu Zhao would displace another concubine who had borne Gaozong a son, as the empress had not. Her plan backfired tragically. Wu Zhao gave the emperor a son in 653 and maneuvered skillfully against both her rivals; she even accused the empress of the murder of Wu Zhao's second child. From 654 to 655, Wu Zhao and the emperor tried to depose Empress Wang so that Wu Zhao could have her position. Respected court advisors opposed their efforts and it was not until November 655 that a key official's view that this was a family matter and not an affair of state served to legitimize their undertaking. Immediately, the empress and the former favorite concubine were accused of trying to poison the emperor, "degraded," and thrown into prison. When the emperor treated the two women kindly even after they were imprisoned, Wu Zhao was infuriated and sent executioners to beat "the two unfortunate women with a hundred blows, cut off their feet and hands, and then throw them, bound, into a brewing vat." When they died several days later, their bodies were decapitated and cut to pieces.[7]

It is reported that Wu Zhao had nightmares about this incident and, in later years, preferred to spend most of her time at Loyang, the "eastern capital," in order to avoid being reminded of her early misdeeds in Chang'an. The new empress was soon able to console herself with power. Her son Li Hong was appointed crown prince in early 656 and within three years all those elder statesmen of the Tang dynasty who had opposed her appointment had been degraded.

After Gaozong suffered a stroke in 660, Wu Zhao conducted the business of state for the next two years. During formal audiences conducted by her husband, she sat behind him and advised him (hidden from petitioners by a screen). Even when healthy, Gaozong had not been a strong ruler; he had apparently let the empress handle many affairs of state because it was easier for him, she was competent, and she used sex to control him. One of the official histories described the situation that existed until Gaozong's death in 683: "The whole sovereign power of the empire passed into her hands; life or death, reward or punishment, were decided by her word. The Son of Heaven sat on his Throne with folded hands, and that was all. Court and country called them the Two Holy Ones."[8]

One of the most interesting features of Empress Wu Zhao's personality was the strong sense of purpose and individuality she displayed. In sharp contrast with Irene, who consistently served the "devout party" in Byzantium, Wu Zhao depended on no one—she served no party, court faction, or family. This self-serving attitude is clear from her treatment of her own family. When her half brother chided her for advancing her mother and blood relatives at court, she decided to teach him a lesson. She told the emperor that it would look better if some of her relatives were transferred to distant posts—and off went her half brother. Sometime later, she killed two birds with one stone by apparently poisoning her niece, who had caught Gaozong's eye, and then blaming the death on her two troublesome nephews, who were then executed.[9] Her behavior contrasted dramatically with that normally expected in a society in which attachment to family was one of life's most important virtues. She did not want to become the pawn of her family, the usual fate of empresses. The price she ultimately paid for her victory was widespread condemnation, much of it deserved, most of it written after her death.

During her lifetime, which encompassed the reigns of her husband and two of her sons, as well as the period from 690 to 705, when she ruled in her own name, would-be critics of Wu Zhao were muted by her ruthless use of power and personal ability. During Gaozong's reign, she used her power over him to arrange the downfall of real or potential opponents. After his death, she ruled through her sons and with the aid of an efficient secret police force which she disbanded once she took sole power.

Wu Zhao was an effective ruler. To call her a decisive administrator is perhaps an understatement, given what we have seen of her style of rule. Yet she combined decisiveness with an intelligent grasp of political problems and the wisdom to employ able administrators who owed their position and power entirely to her. The Chinese empire was peaceful and powerful throughout most of Wu Zhao's reign. She patronized literature and art, and was especially supportive of Buddhism. She established state hospitals and supported scholars at court. Wu Zhao also established a reward and promotion system for state officials, and cut back on expenses for public works in order to save money. In the 670s the empress decreased military expenses but only after she had played an important role in the conquest of Korea in the previous decade. Like her Byzantine counterpart, Wu Zhao lowered taxes for the poor. By the time of his death, Gaozong had so much confidence in Wu Zhao that he asked in his will that his successor defer to her "in all matters pertaining to military and civil affairs."[10]

Wu Zhao and Irene not only shared a concern for reducing taxes on the lower class but also enjoyed at least one other common trait. After holding power in the name of weak male rulers, each decided to rule in her own name. Wu Zhao went even further by deciding to establish a new dynasty, a major change in the Chinese political system. Both women showed considerable patience. It took several years for Irene to arrange the ouster of the son who had severely weakened himself. It took six years, from 684 to 690, for Wu Zhao to plan and execute a change of dynasty. Both women had to find ways to make their power seem legitimate. Irene did this by supporting the "devout party" who favored the use of images. Wu Zhao also used religion. Since imperial power was sacred, Wu Zhao could not simply claim to be "the best person for the job." Heaven—with some aid from her officials—had to sanction so serious a change. In 688 a stone found in the Luo River was said to contain a "mystic inscription" which proclaimed "the Holy Mother has come among men to rule with perpetual prosperity." This clear omen of the need for a change was honored with an elaborate ceremony in which the Luo River was deemed sacred. (While this gave the river no healing qualities, it made fishing in it a sacrilege.) Several years later, after several formal requests from her officials, Wu Zhao announced the end of the Tang dynasty; all members of her own family were given princely rank and her ancestors were posthumously deified. [After her death, however, the Tang dynasty was restored.]

Wu Zhao ruled alone three times longer than Irene—a full fifteen years, despite revolts and intrigues against her. The change of dynasty name made her even more wary of family members who wanted to take power from her during these years. She wanted power for herself; she was not very concerned about the future of her family, or her reputation. Her actions outraged the Confucian scholars, and the bureaucrats bewailed the rule of a woman, especially one who behaved as she did. She caused scandal, for instance, by adopting young men as her favorites at court. Yet the soldiers obeyed orders, the peasants tilled their fields, and people were generally content. It is tempting to suggest that by ruling as successfully as they did, the empresses Wu Zhao and Irene might serve as role models for today's feminists.

At least for a short time, these women challenged the convention that women should not rule a major state. Are they then the spiritual ancestors of the female political leaders of today? The answer must be a qualified no.

Neither Irene nor Wu Zhao saw herself, based upon the evidence we have, as an advocate for women. They clearly wished to secure power for themselves for the same reasons which motivated men. It is interesting that neither the Byzantines nor the Chinese had a term equivalent to our term "empress," which we use to designate a sole woman ruler. Irene signed her decrees as *basilius,* the masculine term for ruler; Wu Zhao was known as "Holy and Divine Emperor" since there was no word in Chinese to indicate a female ruler. Both of these women, like Egyptian Queen Hatshepsut nearly 2000 years earlier, were content to use male titles—as long as they carried the titles and had the power.

This does not mean, however, that these women were not as iconoclastic as some of today's feminists. In the Greek Orthodox tradition, women were to be saintly, and in the Chinese tradition, they were to be submissive. The careers of Irene and Wu Zhao force us to see that these stereotypes do not always reflect reality. Their careers also show that women rulers are capable of crimes as wicked as those we expect only of men. This too helps destroy a stereotype. Irene and Wu Zhao were courageous and capable politicians. In their male-dominated, or patriarchal, society, this was not enough for success. They had to be revolutionaries, for they had to reject the legal and moral restraints of their culture. In the words of Wu Zhao's biographer, C. P. Fitzgerald, women like Wu Zhao were "true revolutionaries" because they had to "repudiate, in their hearts, all the mental barriers which men have built to restrain the use of open violence. The laws, the moralities and the conventions are to women the toys of men; to be played when no essential issue is at stake, but to be cast on one side without a second thought the moment that any really vital need arises."[11]

Fitzgerald's analysis may itself be marred by some traditional Western attitudes about women, most notably the image of women as immoral seductresses that goes back to Eve in the book of Genesis. Perhaps the immoral behavior and the crimes of Irene and Wu Zhao would have been passed over by the historians if these rulers had been male—or if the historians had been female.

Fortunately or unfortunately, depending on your bias, neither was the case.

But if Irene and Wu Zhao were not feminists in the precise modern sense of that term, they were successful female rulers. All modern historians admit the role of Irene in preserving the use of images in Greek Christianity. Wu Zhao did more to preserve Tang power than to destroy it, despite her temporary change of dynasty. Her grandson, Xuanzong, became the most famous Tang ruler, and the Tang period is generally admitted to be the most brilliant in Chinese cultural history. These women were not feminists; they were rulers whose successes compare well with those of modern leaders such as Golda Meir, Margaret Thatcher, or Indira Gandhi. Perhaps if more people knew of the achievements of Irene and Wu Zhao, fewer would be surprised by the rise to power of these twentieth-century female politicians.

Notes

1. *The American Heritage Dictionary of the English Language,* Third Edition (New York: Houghton Mifflin, 1992), 894.
2. Vern L. Bullough, *The Subordinate Sex: A History of Attitudes toward Women* (New York: Penguin Books, 1974), 34–45.
3. Edward Gibbon, *The Decline and Fall of the Roman Empire,* Volume IV (Philadelphia: John C. Winston, 1845), 197. The most hostile of the recent historians is Charles Diehl, author of *Byzantine Empresses,* trans. from the French by Harold Bell and Theresa de Kerpely (New York: Knopf, 1963), chapter IV on Irene, 65–93. Diehl is also author of the pertinent section of Volume IV of the *Cambridge Medieval History* (New York: Macmillan, 1923), "Leo III and the Isaurian Dynasty," 1–26.
4. The *Cambridge Medieval History,* Volume IV, *The Eastern Roman Empire* (New York: Macmillan, 1923), 21.
5. Gibbon, *Decline and Fall,* IV, 197.
6. *Ibid.,* 198.
7. C. P. Fitzgerald, *The Empress Wu,* Second Edition (London: Cresset Press, 1968), 31; to degrade was, literally, to move someone from a higher to a lower grade in the official hierarchy. Often officials who were degraded were sent to the provinces; sometimes they were "accidentally" killed on the way. Our version of degrading, known as demotion, is less severe.
8. From the *T'ung Chien Chi Shih Pen Mo,* quoted in Fitzgerald, *Empress Wu,* 47.
9. Fitzgerald, *Empress Wu,* 49.

10. Nora C. Buckley, "Wu Chao: Woman-Emperor of China," *History Today*, Volume 19 (September 1974), 620. [This spelling of Wu Zhao's name reflects the older Wade-Giles system of transliterating Chinese names into English. It was widely used until recent years.]
11. Fitzgerald, *Empress Wu*, 109.

Further Reading

BUCKLEY, NORA C. "Wu Chao: Woman-Emperor of China," *History Today*, Volume 19 (September 1974), 614–624. Fun to read.

DIEHL, CHARLES. *Byzantine Empresses*, trans. from the French by Harold Bell and Theresa de Kerpely (New York: Knopf, 1963). See chapter IV for his dislike of Irene.

FITZGERALD, C. P. *The Empress Wu*, Second Edition (London: Cresset Press, 1968). Best biography in English; uses Chinese sources extensively.

CHAPTER 7

Genghis Khan: Nomad Conqueror

What did the Asian nomads really want, and what did they accomplish?

He was called "Conqueror of the World"—and for good reason. At his death, the empire of Genghis Khan (1167–1227 AD) stretched 4000 miles from the Pacific Ocean north of Korea to the Crimean peninsula on the Black Sea.[1] His armies were never as large as those of Napoleon or Hitler; they were, for their time, simply better. And, unlike these more famous modern conquerors, Genghis Khan left this world a victor, passing on his empire to his sons and grandsons—who expanded it. One historian has written of this illiterate nomad who never wore a crown and whose remains rest in a secret grave on a north Asian mountainside: "Never before nor since has an army won so many battles, taken so many cities or conquered so many kingdoms."[2]

Who was this man who massacred the inhabitants of entire cities and "made terror a system of government"? How was he able to create such a large empire in such a short time? Finally, what did he wish to accomplish, and what did he accomplish, beyond gaining power for himself?

Ironically for a man whose life caused so much change in world history, Temuchin of the Borjigin clan of Mongols [Genghis Khan was a title] was a traditionalist. After his father was poisoned by Tartars when Temuchin was only twelve, he spent his teenage years supporting his mother and four brothers. During these years he acquired a reputation for bravery and determination by making a daring escape from an enemy tribe that had captured him, and by boldly recapturing eight horses that had been stolen from him. He took his first wife at age sixteen ("when at home he liked to be surrounded by good-looking women"[3]) and soon began to attract to his camp nomadic chieftains who sought a leader who could bring them glory and plunder.

All this, even the conspicuous bravery, was traditional behavior for a person like Temuchin, who was, after all, son of a chieftain. Equally traditional was Temuchin's decision, as a young man, to place himself in the service of Toghrul, the more powerful leader of the neighboring Kerait tribe. We should note that the word "Mongol," which today refers to a large group of people in north and central Asia, referred at that time only to the Mongols proper, or Mangqol people, living between the Onon and Kerulen rivers. It was only after Temuchin had unified all the peoples of Mongolian (and some of Caucasian) racial background in this area—including Keraits, Merkits, Naimans, Uighurs, Oirats, and Tartars—that people acquired the habit of calling the whole group of north and central Asian nomads "Mongols."

In many of these tribes, it was customary for the clan chieftains to select one of their number as a "permanent chief," or khan—if any one of them merited such an honor. The last khan of the Mongols had been Temuchin's great-uncle Kabul. Because of his military skill and leadership ability, Temuchin was named khan by the Mongol nobles when he was in his late twenties. Their statement to him on this occasion, taken from a near-contemporary source, *The Secret History of the Mongols*, gives us some insight into the nomadic philosophy of life:

> We want you to be Khan. If you become Khan, we shall always be foremost in the fight against the foe, and when we take pretty women and girls prisoner, we shall bring them and the best of the loot to you. On the hunt, we shall be before all the others and shall hand over to you the game we strike down. If, in battle, we exceed your orders, or in quiet times, we do you any wrong, take from us our wives and our herds, and drive us into the unpeopled desert.[4]

For his part, of course, the new khan had to lead the nobles and their men to victory and help them get the best women, horses, and game. If he did not or could not do this, the deal was off. This statement tells us what nomadic warriors wanted out of life, and affirms their willingness to follow unquestioningly a leader who would provide them with it. Judging from his later willingness to reward his friends with spoils taken from his enemies, Temuchin never let his people down.

Temuchin's new title did not immediately affect his relationship with Toghrul, who was himself the khan of the Keraits and
who thought it good that the Mongols should have their own khan.
The two continued to fight together against common foes until the
jealousy of Temuchin's boyhood friend Jamuka caused them to become enemies. In the fall of 1203, Temuchin defeated the Keraits
and Toghrul in a battle that was to be a turning point in his career.
He followed it with successful campaigns against the Merkit and
Naiman peoples. Temuchin then sent messages to the remaining
tribes, inviting them to join him. Those who did, according to one
source, were "treated with favor and clemency." Those who resist-
ed "were annihilated until all declared their submission."[5] A new
leader had arisen, even greater than Kabul. In 1206, a general assembly of Mongol chieftains proclaimed Temuchin "Genghis
Khan," a term meaning "universal ruler." The man who began his
career fighting to protect himself and who continued fighting to
avenge his father's death and to bring glory to his clan and tribe
was now undisputed leader of the entire Mongol *ulus*, or peoples.
He had united a people never before united; he had, almost accidentally, burst the bonds of tradition.

Much of the rest of his career is, as they say, history—with a
bit of legend and conjecture thrown in here and there to make it
more interesting. From 1206 to 1209, Genghis Khan [the two
words should not be separated] fought and defeated the Tangut
kingdom in what is today northwestern China. By this time,
Genghis Khan had also secured the allegiance of the Turkish leaders of the Uighur people and of the Kara-Khitai state north of
Tibet. He was now prepared for a showdown with the north Chinese Jin empire—a civilization centered at Beijing that because it
was urban was almost a necessary enemy of "the generations who
lived in felt tents," as the nomads called themselves. The Jin leaders had in the past demanded and received tribute from the Mongol barbarians; in 1210 Genghis Khan felt strong enough to refuse
and between 1211 and 1215 he launched a major campaign against
the Jin. He defeated their forces in the field but was at first unable
to conquer their heavily defended cities. Even after he learned to
use siege works such as catapults, giant crossbows, and pots of
burning naphtha thrown over the walls to start fires, the siege and
sack of Beijing was a major task for the Mongols. Although the Jin
finally recognized Mongol sovereignty, their rule over north China

was not ended and both sides understood that this defeat was a temporary one.

It was in the western, Muslim part of Asia between 1218 and 1224 that Genghis Khan was to earn his reputation for savagery by fighting a "war of annihilation" against the shah of the Khwarizmian empire. This area today includes most of Afghanistan, Iran, and parts of central Asia; at that time it contained the flourishing Muslim cultural centers of Bukhara and Samarkand. The Mongols were at peace with the Turkish Shah Muhammad in 1218 when the Khwarizmian government seized a caravan of Muslim merchants from Mongol-held territory and killed them as spies. When Genghis Khan sent three men to demand that the official who ordered this be released to them for punishment, Muhammad killed the head of the delegation and sent the other two back with their beards shaved, a horrible insult. To punish the shah, Genghis Khan sent an army of over 200,000 men, the largest he ever deployed, into the Khwarizmian empire. Frightened and unwilling to meet the Mongols in open battle, the shah placed most of his army of 300,000 men inside the walls of major cities "where they could be mopped up piecemeal." What happened next caused one Persian Muslim chronicler to lament: "O, would that my mother had never borne me, that I had died and were forgotten. . . . If anyone were to say that at no time since the creation of man by the great God had the world experienced anything like it, he would only be telling the truth."[6]

Genghis Khan usually spared opponents who surrendered without resisting. This trip he made several bloody exceptions to that rule. He burned the town of Balch in Afghanistan and massacred its inhabitants after they surrendered. His son Tuli did the same to the city and people of Merv. The great oasis cities of Bukhara and Samarkand suffered similarly, although they did not resist. The Mongol leader further terrorized the people of Bukhara by calling them together to tell them that he was sent by God to punish them for their sins. It was also during this campaign that Genghis Khan often used enemy prisoners of war as assault troops: Captives from one city were forced to lead the attack on the walls of the next one. After Shah Muhammad died, Mongol troops pursued his successor, Jalal-al-Din, south to the Indus River, where he escaped without his army into the Indian Punjab. This was the only bright spot in the entire war for the Muslim historians, since Jalal-al-Din made his escape by dramatically riding his horse off a cliff into the Indus River.

While destroying the Khwarizmians, Genghis Khan sent two of his most trusted lieutenants into the Caucasus Mountains and southern Russia where they spent the years 1221–1224 camping on the Black Sea, fighting Russians near the mouth of the Dnieper River, and sending spies throughout eastern and central Europe to gather intelligence and spread rumors of Mongol terror, something we call "psychological warfare." Genghis Khan himself fought his last campaign in the East. The revived Jin empire had formed an alliance with the Tangut king, a rebellious vassal of Genghis Khan. Moving south in the winter of 1226, the Mongols defeated the Tangut army on the frozen Yellow River. Final defeat of the Jin eluded him again, but he received the surrender of the Tangut ruler and gave his son Tuli plans for the defeat of the Jin before he died in August 1227. Fifty years later his grandson Kublai Khan would unite *all* of China, including the Song dynasty lands in the south, and establish the Mongol or Yüan dynasty. It is perhaps appropriate, given Genghis Khan's legendary life, that the actual cause of his death should remain a mystery. Some sources say he died of an incurable illness, probably malaria. Another account attributes his death to an act of revenge by the beautiful wife of the Tangut ruler. The least likely story, reported later by Marco Polo, was that he died of an arrow wound to the knee.[7]

How can we explain the success of this greatest of the nomad warriors? Our word "horde," taken from the Mongol *ordu,* meaning camp or field army, suggests a huge body of dirty, undisciplined barbarians, drinking mare's blood, shooting on the run, and defeating their enemies by sheer weight of numbers. Such was not the case. Mongol armies under Genghis Khan *never* outnumbered those of their enemies; they were successful due to "splendid organization, discipline, leadership, and morale."[8] We should add skill, for the Mongols were probably the most skilled horse soldiers of the preindustrial age. They learned to ride their famous ponies at age three, and they began using a bow and arrow at age four or five. The adult Mongol cavalryman could shoot an arrow with deadly accuracy over a hundred yards; he could do this riding full gallop and even, when necessary, when retreating and shooting over his shoulder; a high saddle and stirrups (a Mongol invention later adopted in the West) kept him from falling. Mongol armies could ride for days without stopping to cook food. They carried kumis, dried milk curd, cured meat, and water, and could eat, drink, and sleep on horseback. On long trips, they relied on the land of the enemy to support them. In 1221, for example, Genghis Khan tested the endurance of his men by chasing Jalal-al-Din 130 miles through the mountains of Afghanistan in two days.[9] The feat surpasses even the formidable forced marches of Napoleon 600 years later.

Without the skill and endurance of individual Mongol cavalrymen, the armies of Genghis Khan would have been harder to organize. But as it was, organization and discipline became the key to the victories of the Great Khan. Before one battle, Genghis Khan issued the following order: "If during an attack or retreat a soldier's baggage, bow, or saddle falls to the ground and the warrior behind him rides on without dismounting to help, that warrior will be executed."[10] Genghis Khan used a traditional decimal organization. Divisions, or *toumen*, of 10,000 men were divided into regiments of 1000; these were then subdivided into squads of 100 and patrols, or *arban*, of ten men each. Each unit commander gave strict obedience to his superior, on pain of death. In campaigns, *toumens* could travel in widely separated columns and unite quickly in battle. During winter Genghis Khan drilled his men with hunts conducted as military exercises, more real than modern "war games." For Mongols, fighting on horseback was a way of life, not something they did only when attacked. They were a mounted nation.

Genghis Khan was also gifted with great shrewdness. His military code specified that a man who was physically stronger than his comrades was not to be placed in command of them "because he could not feel hunger and thirst as they did and would thus reduce their efficiency."[11] To curb drunkenness among his troops, Genghis Khan decreed in his code that a man could only get drunk three times a month. "Twice is better than three times; once is better still, and the best of all is never to drink," he added, "but who can find a man who will never get drunk?"[12] The Mongol leader was equally shrewd in dealing with his enemies. His armies became famous for their tricks, such as pretending to retreat and then returning with fresh horses to engulf their surprised pursuers, or tying branches on their ponies' tails to raise a cloud of dust that made it seem they had more men. Perhaps this helps explain the frequently exaggerated estimates of Mongol troop strength in some contemporary reports. The following story, probably legendary, suggests the ingenuity attributed to Genghis Khan. In 1207, before he had learned siege tactics, the Mongol leader was having trouble taking the Tangut town of Volohai. In apparent despair, he is supposed to have said that he would leave if the defenders gave him 1000 cats and 10,000 swallows as tribute. Puzzled, they did so. The Mongols then tied "cottonwool" to the tails of the birds and cats, lit them, and released them to fly or run back into the town. While the defenders were fighting the fires, the Mongols overran the city.[13]

Despite these forms of deception, as well as his use of merchants as spies (also an old nomad custom) and the spreading of what today is called "disinformation," the major reason for the success of the nomad chieftain was the speed and skill of his soldiers and their unwillingness to give up. They were as tireless in pursuit as they were savage in victory. Both demoralize any enemy. One student of Mongol history has suggested that Mongol military tactics, particularly their emphasis on endurance, speed, and the use of flanking movements to encircle their enemies, were natural outgrowths of the tactics of any hunter on the Asian steppelands. Stalking deer silently taught them how to stalk men; using a line of beaters to head off and terrify a circle of game taught them how to outflank their foes. They surprised their enemies, human or animal. In both cases, they generally killed them after capture. This was the way of the steppe, and they were steppe hunters.[14]

Whether this was the reason for their success or not, there is no doubt that Genghis Khan and his people ride out of history as some of the most successful warriors of all time. He was driven by a desire for power, and his armies have a record of accomplishment on the battlefield easily equal to those of Alexander the Great or any of the Roman Caesars; his system of military government and command may have been unmatched until the twentieth century. All this, of course, must be balanced against the savagery of his troops, especially during the western campaign. Some scholars have tried to excuse or explain the brutality of the Mongols by pointing out that their cruelty was not "wanton," but only the product of their culture. Genghis Khan did not kill his opponents out of blood lust, they argue, but only as a matter of policy. One scholar, David Morgan, wrote that Genghis Khan's principle in destroying some cities was similar to the one used by President Truman when he decided to drop the atomic bomb on the Japanese cities of Hiroshima and

Nagasaki in 1945: If the inhabitants of several cities were massacred, those in other cities would be less likely to resist.[15] Such arguments as these mean little to those who have been destroyed, but they do begin to raise the question of whether or not the career of Genghis Khan has any "redeeming historical value" for anyone other than the military historian. When you subtract the savagery and military success, what is left?

At least two things are left. First, however brutally he may have done it, Genghis Khan did unify the Asian steppelands, and in doing this he opened a corridor of cultural, commercial, and technological interchange between east Asia and Europe that had been closed since the fall of the Han dynasty in China and the Roman empire in the West some 700 years earlier. Marco Polo was only the most famous European who traveled this corridor during the century and a half that it was open. Christian missionaries went east while silk and spices once again moved overland to the West. There were only two periods in world history before the western voyages of exploration when the eastern and western ends of the Eurasian continent were linked. The second and most important of these two periods was due to the work of Genghis Khan. It was only, in fact, because this overland route was closed by the decline of the Mongol khanates during the fifteenth century that men like Prince Henry the Navigator and Columbus began to look for a sea route to the East—and we all know where that led.

There is a second reason for reserving a place in our histories for Genghis Khan. He does give us an insight into the values of the nomads, and this understanding itself, while interesting to us, was a matter of life and death for the inhabitants of most urban civilizations for the first 4000 years of recorded history. Genghis Khan disliked cities, or the agricultural and urban economy that we generally regard as one of the essentials of civilized life. There is a famous story (this one not legend) that during his last campaign in China, one of the Mongol generals suggested that Genghis Khan should exterminate the ten million Chinese under his control. After all, they were unsuited to warfare, and most were poor horsemen. The Great Khan initially liked the idea of turning northern China into a pasture, until his patient and trusted Chinese advisor, Yelü Chucai, explained to the conqueror that he could tax the ten million and get much silver, silk, and grain each year by doing so. After thinking about it for a moment, Genghis Khan agreed.

Nomads saw cities not as bases for control of the countryside and further conquest but first, as obstacles, and second, as sources of wealth. The cities that Genghis Khan did not destroy, he allowed to exist only because they could supply him with tribute. The Mongol ruler saw his empire not as a great world state but as a resource for his people so that they could continue to enjoy the morally superior life of the steppes for uncounted generations. The cities in the south would supply them with money and slaves so that they could enjoy unhindered the free and open life of "the generations who live in felt tents." It did not work out quite that way. Although the great Mongol empire grew under the leadership of his sons and grandsons, Genghis Khan's nomads eventually split into separate groups, and each one was attracted by the lure of the sedentary, urban civilization over which it ruled. Grandson Kublai Khan became a Chinese emperor while grandson Hulegu became a Persian prince.

The Mongol *ulus* of Genghis Khan eventually became civilized, and in the process, many lost the art of riding while shooting arrows long distances. Yet despite the cruelty that inspired fear in the hearts of European Christians, Persian Muslims, and Chinese Confucians, and despite the ultimate failure of his empire to remain what he wished it to be, the legend of this great world conqueror lives on. Eight hundred years after he was first made leader of his people, modern-day Mongols have named a vodka and a hotel for him.[16] And he will remain a legend, for he is one of only a handful of historical individuals whose actions have affected the lives of so many people, over such a wide area, in such a short period of time.

Notes

1. His actual date of birth is in dispute and his name, like almost all Mongol terms, is spelled in a variety of ways in English sources. The alcoholic beverage made from fermented mare's milk is koumiss, kumis, or kumiss; the main wife of Genghis Khan has five names, perhaps a record. She is called Börte, Borte, Bortei, Berta, and Burte.
2. H. Desmond Martin, *The Rise of Chingis Khan and His Conquest of North China* (Baltimore: Johns Hopkins Press, 1950), 44. One story tells of Genghis Khan being buried with much treasure, carried to the burial site by 2000 servants, who were butchered at the site to keep the location secret. The 4000 soldiers who murdered the first 2000 were themselves slaughtered by 15,000 other soldiers when they arrived back at

the capital. See Idelle Davidson, "The Wealth of Khan," *American Way*, July 15, 1991, 34–38.

3. Boris I. Vladimirtsov, *The Life of Chingis-Khan* (Boston: Houghton Mifflin, 1930), 155; Paul Ratchnevsky, *Genghis Khan: His Life and Legacy* (Cambridge, MA: Basil Blackwell, 1992), 18–19.

4. Michael Prawdin, *The Mongol Empire: Its Rise & Legacy*, Second Edition (New York: Free Press, 1967), 50.

5. Ratchnevsky, *Genghis Khan: Life and Legacy*, 82.

6. Bertold Spuler, *History of the Mongols: Based on Eastern and Western Accounts of the Thirteenth and Fourteenth Centuries* (Berkeley: University of California Press, 1972), 29–30; David Morgan, *The Mongols* (Oxford: Basil Blackwell, 1986), 68–69.

7. Ratchnevsky, *Genghis Khan: Life and Legacy*, 141–142.

8. Martin, *The Rise of Chingis Khan*, 16.

9. *Ibid.*, 18.

10. Ratchnevsky, *Genghis Khan: Life and Legacy*, 190.

11. E. D. Phillips, *The Mongols* (London: Thames and Hudson, 1969), 45.

12. Vladimirtsov, *Life of Chingis-Khan*, 59–60.

13. Peter Brent, *Genghis Khan: The Rise, Authority and Decline of Mongol Power* (New York: McGraw-Hill, 1976), 48.

14. René Grousset, *Empire of the Steppes: A History of Central Asia* (New Brunswick, NJ: Rutgers University Press, 1970), 224–225.

15. Morgan, *The Mongols*, 93.

16. See Nicholas Kristof, "Where Genghis Khan Is In," *New York Times*, May 27, 1990, 20; John Noble Wilford, "Buddha and Genghis Khan Back in Mongolia," *New York Times*, July 22, 1991, 1, 7.

Further Reading

GROUSSET, RENÉ. *Empire of the Steppes: A History of Central Asia* (New Brunswick, NJ: Rutgers University Press, 1970). Good, short treatment of a broad subject; see 189–252 on Genghis Khan.

MORGAN, DAVID. *The Mongols* (Oxford: Basil Blackwell, 1986). Readable scholarly work which compares and evaluates the works of many other scholars.

PRAWDIN, MICHAEL. *The Mongol Empire: Its Rise & Legacy* (New York: Free Press, 1967). Short, scholarly, readable.

CHAPTER 8

Marco Polo and Ibn Battuta: The Merchant and the Pilgrim

How did the predispositions of two famous medieval travelers color what they reported—and how they reported it?

Today the word "travel" carries with it images of excitement: We can move hundreds of miles by automobile or thousands of miles by air in a few hours. When we arrive at our destination, we can usually relax comfortably in a home or motel.

Such was not the case seven centuries ago, when the English word "travel" originally meant the same as "travail," that is, hard work that would exhaust the body and test the will.[1] Imagine how stressful it would be to live "out of a suitcase" for over twenty years and in the process risk serious illnesses and survive dangers posed by bandits, shipwrecks, pirates, trackless deserts, and frozen mountains.

These were only some of the problems faced by the two most famous world travelers in the premodern period. In 1271 the Italian Marco Polo (1254–1324) set out with his father and uncle on a journey to the court of the Mongol Emperor of China Kublai Khan; he would not return to his native Venice until 1295. In 1325, a year after Polo's death, the Islamic jurist Ibn Battuta (1304–1368) left his native city of Tangier in Morocco to begin a journey to the East that would take him a total of 75,000 miles; he did not return home permanently until 1354.[2]

The thirteenth-century travels of Marco Polo and those of his fourteenth-century Muslim counterpart Ibn Battuta illustrate both the dangers travel posed in this period and how such dangers could be overcome. The Polo family was aided by the "Pax Mongolica," the period of peace established by Mongol rulers in the Asian steppelands from about 1250 to 1350. The strong control exercised by these rulers, in an empire which stretched from Persia to China, allowed the Polos safe passage to China and back. Fifty years later, when Ibn Battuta began his journey, the Pax Mongolica was more precarious, but hospitality and safety were provided to Muslims by a network of Muslim traders and rulers extending from southeast Asia to the strait of Gibraltar.

Ibn Battuta traveled primarily in Muslim-ruled lands, the *Dar al-Islam* [House or Abode of Islam], while the Christian Polo, son of a European merchant, lived and worked in countries whose cultures and religions were foreign to him. This difference makes a comparison of their works most interesting. Marco Polo's knowledge of four Asian languages as well as Italian allowed him to communicate with foreigners and even work as an administrator for the Chinese emperor. Yet in all his travels, he remained culturally an "outsider" to the peoples he met, and this fact enhanced his power of observation and stimulated his natural curiosity. By contrast, Ibn Battuta usually traveled as an "insider" and his hosts accepted him as a respected Muslim jurist *(qadi)* and student of Islamic mysticism (Sufism). Traveling to over sixty Muslim courts where he met rulers and their officials, Ibn Battuta was able to judge the behavior of his hosts in light of the Muslim scripture, the Koran, and the precepts of Islamic law. For him the difference between their native cultures and his own north Arabic culture was of secondary importance.

We can be thankful that both men dictated accounts of their travels after they returned home—Polo, while in a Genoese prison in 1298, and Ibn Battuta, to a Moroccan scribe, Ibn Juzayy, in 1354–1355. Since neither was trained to report objectively on the unusual customs of foreigners, both Polo and Ibn Battuta judged those they encountered by their own standards. Both travel accounts reveal the great diversity in Eurasian cultures during this period; both are laced with "miraculous" happenings and both amaze readers with fairly accurate accounts of the enormous wealth rulers had at their disposal. The chief difference between the two works is one of focus. Polo's *Travels* was written with a "merchant's eye for flourishing manufactures." It is marked, in the words of one biographer, with a "mercantile stamp."[3] Polo tells us little about himself but much about the social and economic practices of those he meets. He systematically discusses commerce, government, and customs with some attention to the spectacular and exotic. By contrast, Ibn Battuta focused on the purity of Islamic ritual and belief in the lands he visited. He was much more willing than was Polo to describe his own difficulties and good fortune, and much less concerned with trade, commerce, and the forms of government. Ibn Battuta's *Rihla* (Arabic for *Travels*) described a personal journey, a pilgrimage. Indeed, Ibn Battuta began his journey intending to make only the pilgrimage to Mecca *(hadj)* required of all pious Muslims once in a lifetime.

Although Polo infused his *Travels* with a "mercantile spirit," he left Palestine in 1271 with a religious purpose. On an earlier journey to China, Marco's father Nicolo and his uncle Maffeo had been asked by the Great Khan (Kublai) to bring back to the Mongol court some holy oil from Jerusalem and "a hundred men of learning, thoroughly acquainted with the principles of the Christian religion," who could make a case for Christianity. Kublai may have wished to compare the "wonders" of Christian priests with those of the holy men of other religions; evidence suggests, however, that his mother was a Christian, and his requests could reflect a genuine interest in learning more about her faith.[4] Western Christian leaders, for their part, hoped to convert the Mongols to Christianity and use them as allies against the "infidel" Muslim Turks, whose lands lay between Christian Europe and China. Although such hopes were unrealistic, Pope Gregory X supplied the Polos with two priests and some oil from Jerusalem's shrine of the Holy Sepulchre; the priests, fearing attack, abandoned the Polos after traveling only a few hundred miles.

Without the priests, but with the oil and valuable "safe conduct" passes earlier provided by the khan, the Polos crossed Asia Minor and reached the Persian city of Tabriz in 1272. From there they headed south to Hormuz on the Persian Gulf to take a ship to southeast Asia and China. However, when they discovered that the Arab ships were held together with rope yarn instead of nails, they decided to travel overland through central Asia (Afghanistan and Tibet).

In Baku, southwest of the Caspian Sea, Polo encountered his first natural wonder, petroleum, which was used "as an unguent for the cure of rashes in men and cattle . . . and [was] . . . also good for burning." On the road to Hormuz, he encountered—as did Ibn Battuta decades later—the *simoon*, or "drying wind" of the desert, which not only could suffocate men but also dry out their corpses so that their limbs would fall off when men tried to remove them for burial.[5] While traveling through the Pamir Mountains and

the Gobi Desert, the Polo party encountered the hardships associated with travels in thinly populated lands. In eastern Afghanistan,
Marco fell ill and took a full year to recover; this is one of the few
times in the *Travels* that he mentions his personal misfortunes. After
leaving the city of Balach, the Polos entered a country where the
people had fled to the mountains to escape bandits. As a consequence local provisions were scarce and travelers had to carry
enough food with them for themselves and their cattle. In the Pamir
Mountains, the Polos saw no birds and noticed that their fires gave
less heat because they were 15,600 feet above sea level. The Gobi
Desert seemed to the Polos a place of hallucinations, "the abode of
many evil spirits which lure travelers to their destruction with the
most extraordinary illusions."[6]

The Polos were relieved once they left the Gobi and entered the
northern Chinese province of Tangut (Gansu). There the party safe-
ly spent over a year and the Polos had ample time to observe
provincial customs and the many religions of the people: Some of
them were Saracens [Muslim], some were Nestorian Christian, and
some were "idolaters" [Buddhists]. For the first time Polo came
upon a new fibre (asbestos) which "when woven into cloth and
thrown in the fire . . . does not burn." But what fascinated the
young traveler most were the marriage and sexual customs of the
Asians. He recorded that in Pem in central Asia, a woman could
take another husband if her first husband was absent from home
twenty days. "On the same principle," he added, men "marry
wherever they happen to reside." In places, Polo found men willing
to offer wives and daughters to strangers passing through. They believed this practice was "agreeable to their deities" and would
bring them wealth and good fortune. The women, he added know-
ingly, were "very handsome, very sensual."[7]

Polo described most of these customs in a matter-of-fact tone.
In one southeast Asian land he later visited, he calmly reported that
no young woman could be married until "she has first been tried
by the king." If the king liked her, he kept her around for a time,
then dismissed her with a sum of money that would allow her to
make an "advantageous match" within her class. Polo also noted
that the king had 326 children. However, Polo was personally offended by a custom he encountered in Kanchow, China. There men
took as many as thirty wives and often married close relatives, even
mothers-in-law. Polo considered this "like the beasts of the field."

He also described as "scandalous" the Tibetan dislike of virgins; they expected unmarried girls to "have had previous relations with many of the opposite sex." This practice of judging a woman attractive on the basis of "the number of lovers she had" was due, he believed, to Tibetan paganism.[8]

Polo did appreciate the strict marriage customs of the Mongols, which contrasted sharply with those of other Asians. Mongol women "excelled in chastity and decency of conduct," he wrote, and husbands remained loyal to their wives, though they could have as many of them as they could afford.[9] Although Marco Polo worked for Kublai Khan for seventeen years, some of his praise of the Mongols strains our credibility. It might be appropriate to call this ruler a "man of proved integrity, great wisdom, commanding eloquence, and celebrated valor," but to say that he was so virtuous that "wherever he went he found people disposed to submit to him" is carrying admiration a bit far.[10] Generally, however, Polo's account of the history, military organization, and social customs of the Mongols was accurate, even though his description of the khan's court and its activities may have been exaggerated. Polo's European readers would later have trouble believing Polo's statement that Kublai Khan kept a stud farm of 10,000 horses and mares, all "white as snow." They were also skeptical of Polo's claim that the khan hunted with 10,000 falconers and hosted a state dinner so large that 40,000 people had to eat outside the hall. Yet, when one considers the size of the Mongol empire, of which China was only a part, Polo's estimates might be only slightly exaggerated. It is quite possible, despite the ridicule of Venetians, who referred to Marco as "il Milione," the man who speaks in millions, that Kublai Khan's postal system (something like the American pony express) used 200,000 horses to supply 10,000 stations across Asia. It is also quite possible that the city of Hangchow included 1,600,000 families and that some Tibetan monasteries housed up to 500 monks.[11]

Marco Polo saw much of China when he was sent by the khan on two long inspection tours, the first southwest through the modern provinces of Sichuan and Yunnan into Burma and the second southeast from Khanbaliq, the site of modern Beijing, to the coastal cities of Kinsai and Zaiton (modern Hangchow and Amoy). In describing these trips, as well as the journey home by sea through southeast Asia and along the Indian coast, Polo's reporting followed a pattern. He opened with an account of the religion, government, and economic and commercial activity of the peoples he encountered. For example, he noted that in the city of Nanjing, China, "the people are idolaters [Buddhists], use paper money . . . are subjects of the Great Khan, and are largely engaged in commerce. They have raw silk, and weave tissues of silver and gold. . . . The country produces a great deal of corn [grain]." Later, in discussing the island of Sumatra, Polo wrote:

> In this island there are eight kingdoms, each governed by its own king, and each with its own language. The people are idolaters. It contains an abundance of riches and all sorts of spices, aloes wood, sapanwood for dyeing, and various other kinds of drugs, which, on account of the length of the voyage and the danger . . . are not imported into our country, but which find their way to the provinces of Manzi [south China] and Cathay [north China].[12]

Polo's account of conditions in Kinsai (Hangchow) was particularly detailed. The city had a perimeter of a hundred miles, contained ten large marketplaces, and possessed paved roads that were guarded by watchmen on the lookout for fires. Polo was very impressed with both the well-organized government and the wealth of this trading center. On the door of his home, each head of household in Kinsai had to list the names of family members and the number of horses owned so that authorities could keep constant track of city growth. The wealth of the city is suggested by the amount of pepper brought daily to the city; 43 boatloads, each weighing 243 pounds, arrived daily. Kublai Khan took in millions in revenue from this one city alone.[13]

Despite Marco Polo's focus on imports, exports, and local industries within the confines of Eurasia, he remained a child of his age—an age when people in every culture were fascinated with "miracles" and "wonders." One critic suggests that Polo preferred to write about the "popular culture" of everyday life rather than the "high culture" of Asia because he himself was culturally unsophisticated.[14] Polo never discussed art, philosophy, or literature, for example, but enjoyed mentioning such things as tattooing and cannibalism. While Polo did uncritically repeat stories of the miraculous, it is also true that most of his readers in fourteenth-century Europe believed them. They enjoyed his story of the one-eyed cobbler who saved the Christians in Baghdad from certain death by accepting a challenge from the Muslim caliph, praying, and moving a mountain. Polo's Christian readers were edified by his story of how the Church of St. John the Baptist in Samarkand remained standing after Christians complied with the order of the Muslim ruler to remove a portion of a central supporting pillar. These miracle stories are more credible than other Polo tales based on sheer fantasy: the existence of two islands 500 miles south of India, one inhabited only by males, and another thirty miles away inhabited only by females, or of birds on Madagascar large enough to pick up elephants in their talons and drop them on rocks to kill them.[15]

It is interesting that both Polo and his Muslim counterpart, Ibn Battuta, noted some of the same marvels during their journeys. How must contemporaries have viewed stories of dog sleds in Siberia, the practice of suttee in Hindu India [widows throwing themselves on their husbands' funeral pyres], or the burning of strange black stones (coal) to heat houses?[16] These things must have seemed as strange to the people of the fourteenth century as moving mountains by prayer does to us.

The Polo party left China in 1292, charged by the emperor with delivering a new wife to Arghun, khan of Persia. Supplied with large ships and many servants, the Polos took twenty-one months to complete their journey because of a five-month delay on the island of Sumatra. During the trip nearly 600 members of the party died from various unspecified causes, but Marco Polo, his father, and his uncle finally returned to Venice, where they ended their lives as ordinary merchants.[17]

Ibn Battuta's journey, begun thirty years later, took him to more places than the Polos had visited. After leaving his home in the Moroccan coastal town of Tangier in 1325, Ibn Battuta wandered through the Nile valley and Syria and arrived in Mecca in 1326 for the first of four pilgrimages to that holy city. During the next year, he visited Persia (then a Mongol state) and Iraq but returned to Mecca to engage in further study and religious meditation. Between 1328 and 1332 Ibn Battuta sailed southward down the east African coast to Kilwa and then turned back to visit Turkey, the Crimea, southern Russia, and the city of Constantinople. In 1333 he was in India, where he spent a number of years as the *qadi*, or Muslim judge, of Delhi. This largely honorific post paid well but also required him to spend much of his own money. Soon Ibn Battuta had a dangerous falling-out with the sultan of Delhi which nearly cost him his life; he returned to favor in 1341 when he was asked by the sultan to head a delegation to the emperor of China. Because of further adventures along the Malabar (west) coast of India and in the Maldive Islands and Ceylon (Sri Lanka), the ambassador did not arrive in China until 1345, where he spent most of his time in the south. Between 1346 and 1349, the Arab jurist returned via Mecca to Tunis in north Africa and during the next five years he crossed the Sahara to visit Mali, a black African Islamic state in the western Sudan. In 1354 he returned to Morocco, where he completed dictating his *Travels* by December 1355.[18]

Since Ibn Battuta was a pilgrim, the central theme which marks his narrative is the insistence that one must live a properly pious Muslim life. He expected his fellow Muslims to be devout in attending prayer services, keep their women modest, and show hospitality to strangers.

In his travels, Ibn Battuta liked to visit with Islamic holy men (pious *shaykhs*) and view the tombs of holy men. In Cairo, Ibn Battuta visited the "great cemetery of al-Qarafa . . . a place of particular sanctity" containing "the graves of innumerable scholars and pious believers." At Hebron he discovered the graves of Abraham, Isaac, and Jacob, and their respective wives.[19] The bad grammar used by a preacher at Basra near the Persian Gulf bothered him, but he was glad that the Khwarizmians in central Asia beat people who failed to show up for Friday prayer service. During periods of crisis, or while waiting to begin another leg of his journey, Ibn Battuta spent hours, even days, reciting the *Koran*. When serving as *qadi* in the Maldive Islands, he had those who missed prayer services beaten; he also tried to get women to dress modestly, but they refused to cover themselves completely except when they were in his court.[20]

Throughout the *Rihla*, Ibn Battuta carefully noted which rulers and officials respected his status as a pilgrim and extended hospitality to him. Indeed, without the generosity of his hosts he could not have continued traveling. Sultan Abu Sa'id of Iraq gave him a robe, a horse, and other provisions when he found out that Ibn Battuta was going to Mecca. One of the ruler's wives in Qaysariya in Iraq gave Ibn Battuta's party a meal and then presented him with a horse, with saddle and bridle, and money. In western Turkey, he stayed with a sultan who "every night sent us food, fruit, sweetmeats, and candles, and gave me in addition a hundred pieces of gold [and] a complete set of garments. . . ." The Sultan Abu 'l-Muzaffar Hasan at Kilwa was also praised for "his gifts and generosity"; this leader devoted "the fifth part of the booty made on his expeditions to pious and charitable purposes, as is prescribed in the *Koran*, and I have seen him give the clothes off his back to a mendicant who asked for them."[21]

Except for those times when he had been robbed or shipwrecked, Ibn Battuta traveled in style. He customarily journeyed with slaves of both sexes, many of them gifts to him or to his companions. While in Afghanistan, Ibn Battuta reported that his party "had about 4000 horses" as well as some camels. When sent to China as ambassador of the sultan of Delhi, Ibn Battuta took gifts of 100 horses, 200 slaves and dancing girls, fifteen eunuchs [castrated males], 1200 pieces of cloth, gold, silver, and other assorted presents. When Ibn Battuta visited "Adam's Foot," a mountain in Ceylon (modern Sri Lanka) revered by Hindus, Buddhists, and Muslims, he received an escort of four Hindu yogis, three Brahman priests, ten guards, and fifteen men to carry provisions.[22]

Ibn Battuta shared his personality with his readers more readily than did Marco Polo, and his text suggests he was a reasonably complex person. A lover of religious truth, correct ritual, and dogma, Ibn Battuta was also "fond of pleasure and uxorious" [inclined to dote on someone]. A recent scholar notes his "well-timed unctuousness" [excessively pious, smooth, or oily manner] and suggests that he may have wanted rulers to treat him with great honor because in fact he felt insecure about his own level of learning and legal abilities. While serving as a *qadi* in Delhi, for example, he was untrained in the particular school of law practiced there and could not even speak the language.[23] If it is true that this world traveler was personally insecure, it is remarkable that he tells us as much about his personal life as he does. He did not hide the fact that he flattered rulers in return for their money and favors. Yet Ibn Battuta was not a cynical politician but, like Marco Polo, a genuinely curious person who loved travel for its own sake and who could be sincerely generous and open with people. On the two chief occasions when he got into trouble with rulers, at Delhi and in the Maldive Islands, he attempted to play a political role for which he was unsuited. It is not surprising that he retreated to the life of a hermit after his narrow escape in Delhi and that he reentered the sultan's service to head the embassy to China because of his "love of travel and sight-seeing."[24]

Like Marco Polo, Ibn Battuta loved to share his experiences with the readers; he too saw oil in Iraq and pearl divers in the Indian Ocean. He described the way Arab ships were built in the Persian Gulf and contrasted them with Chinese ships on which he later traveled. The strangest thing he saw was a slave in southeast Asia who gave a long flattering speech before his ruler and then cut his own throat—as a way of showing his great love for the sultan. This demonstration of loyalty was rewarded, for his family was given a large pension.[25]

The different personalities of Polo and Ibn Battuta are reflected in quite different styles of reporting. For example, in his accounts of the city of Quilon on the west coast of India, Polo the merchant commented on the amount of dyewood and fruit as well as on the palm wine that "makes one drunk faster than the wine from grapes." He also noted the inhabitants' nakedness, except for a loincloth, and the fact that they marry close relatives. Ibn Battuta, by contrast, told the reader little about the flora, fauna, or people of Quilon. We are told that he arrived there after missing a ship in Calicut and losing nearly all his possessions; the most memorable thing about Quilon for Ibn Battuta was the quarrelsome, drunken porter who took him there from Calicut.[26]

As this example illustrates, while there is more ego evident in the *Rihla* than we find in Polo's *Travels*, Ibn Battuta's book contains more detailed cultural information and more exciting stories. Nowhere in Polo's book, for example, can one find a story to rival Ibn Battuta's account of how he escaped near-death from bandits as he was leaving Delhi on his mission to China. After being pursued by ten horsemen and outrunning them, he was then captured by forty bowmen and taken to their camp where several men were assigned to kill him. His assassins lost their nerve, however, and allowed him to escape after he gave one of them (literally) the shirt off his back. He then wandered the countryside for six days, at one point eluding a band of fifty armed Hindus by hiding in a cotton field all day, until a kindly Muslim found him, took him home, and sent word to the members of his party, who returned and picked him up.[27] This close brush with death is only one of a half dozen reported in the *Rihla*; whether caused by illness, pirates, treacherous guides, stormy seas, or crocodiles, they are all presented believably but dramatically in the narrative.[28]

Both the merchant and the pilgrim give us a clear appreciation of how travelers, whether Christian or Muslim, merchant or jurist, viewed the world in the later medieval period. For both men, the world was a truly marvelous and sometimes miraculous place where fact and fantasy intermingled in a way we find incomprehensible today. Even though they are not always reliable witnesses and were not writing history as we understand that term, both world travelers are praised by modern scholars for the practical information they recorded. In his book *The Discoverers*, historian Daniel Boorstin says of Marco Polo's book: "Never before or since has a single book brought so much authentic new information, or so widened the vistas for a continent." Other authors mention that a well-thumbed and annotated copy of Polo's *Travels* was found in Christopher Columbus's private library; the book may have helped Columbus decide to sail west to reach Asia because it describes Japan as a good 1500 miles east of China. That would have placed it about where the Americas are located—if we take into account the smaller globe that Columbus would have used. Ibn Battuta's *Rihla* gives us the only information we have on many Muslim states in this period, especially those in west Africa and along the west coast of India.[29] Yet, despite the practical value of these two travel works, we should remember that they were written to entertain and to edify. Although Polo's work excited Europeans on the eve of an era of discovery and exploration, and Ibn Battuta's work confirmed for Muslims the essential religious unity of the *Dar al-Islam*, each man wrote to please himself and charm his readers. That, as much as the information they contain, is what makes these two travel narratives interesting reading today.

Notes

1. Daniel J. Boorstin, *The Discoverers* (New York: Random House, 1983), 125.
2. Ibn Battuta's full name was Abu 'Abdallah Muhammad ibn Abdallah ibn Muhammad ibn Ibrahim al-Lawati ibn Battuta. In Arabic, "ibn" means "son of" and Lawata was the name of his particular Berber tribe; see Ross E. Dunn, *The Adventures of Ibn Battuta: A Muslim Traveler of the 14th Century* (Berkeley: University of California Press, 1986), 19.
3. *The Travels of Marco Polo*, edited with an introduction by Milton Rugoff (New York: New American Library, 1961), xxv; Richard Humble, *Marco Polo* (New York: G. P. Putnam's Sons, 1975), 55.

4. *Travels of Marco Polo*, 39; Henry H. Hart, *Marco Polo: Venetian Adventurer* (Norman: University of Oklahoma Press, 1967), 38–39; Humble, *Marco Polo*, 37–38.

5. *Travels of Marco Polo*, 51, 69; see H. A. R. Gibb, trans., *Ibn Battuta: Travels in Asia and Africa, 1325–1354* (London: George Rutledge and Sons, 1929), 120.

6. *Travels of Marco Polo*, 77, 81, 83–84, 89; Humble, *Marco Polo*, 85, 94.

7. *Ibid.*, 94–95, 87, 93, 177–178; the Nestorians were declared heretics in the fifth century in a dispute over the nature of Christ. They established churches throughout Asia at this time.

8. *Ibid.*, 96–97, 175, 236.

9. *Ibid.*, 103.

10. *Ibid.*, 99; for more on Marco Polo's loyalty to the Mongol dynasty, see Leonardo Olschki, *Marco Polo's Asia* (Berkeley: University of California Press, 1960), 316–317, 397–404.

11. *Ibid.*, 115, 117, 148, 156, 220; Humble, *Marco Polo*, 124, 206.

12. *Travels of Marco Polo*, 202–203, 238.

13. *Ibid.*, 209–221; Humble, *Marco Polo*, 160–164.

14. Olschki, *Marco Polo's Asia*, 145.

15. *Travels of Marco Polo*, 57–59, 85–86, 268.

16. Dunn, *Adventures of Ibn Battuta*, 314–316; Gibb, *Ibn Battuta's Travels*, 150, 191–192; *Travels of Marco Polo*, 161, 249.

17. *Travels of Marco Polo*, xxi–xxiii; Humble, *Marco Polo*, 191–206; Hart, *Marco Polo*, 159–160.

18. For a brief account of Ibn Battuta's itinerary, see 2–8 of Gibb, *Ibn Battuta's Travels*. There is a dispute among scholars concerning just how much time Ibn Battuta spent in Mecca during his second visit. He claims he was there until 1330, but that would give him insufficient time to reach India by 1333 and visit all the places he said he visited before arriving in India. The dates used in this essay are ones suggested, on the basis of evidence in the *Travels* themselves, by Ross E. Dunn; see his *Adventures of Ibn Battuta*, 106 and notes on 132–133 and 181–182.

19. Gibb, *Ibn Battuta: Travels*, 51, 55.

20. *Ibid.*, 87, 168, 239, 243–244, 250.

21. *Ibid.*, 101–102, 131, 134, 112.

22. *Ibid.*, 180, 214, 258; see also 152, 236, 246–247, and Dunn, *Adventures*, 165, 177, for other examples of gifts given to Ibn Battuta and for examples of his desire to travel in comfort.

23. Gibb, *Ibn Battuta: Travels*, 2; Dunn, *Adventures*, 149, 311–312.

24. Dunn, *Adventures*, 197–209, 238–239; Gibb, *Ibn Battuta: Travels*, 212–213; Lucile McDonald, *The Arab Marco Polo* (Nashville: Thomas Nelson, 1975), 122–135; see also Ivan Hrbek, "Ibn Battutah," *Encyclopaedia Britannica*, Volume 9 (Chicago: Benton, 1974), 144–145.

25. McDonald, *Arab Marco Polo*, 37, 49; *Travels of Marco Polo*, 228–229, 247; Gibb, *Ibn Battuta: Travels*, 121–122, 235–236, 243, 177, 268–269, 277–278.

26. *Travels of Marco Polo*, 259–260; Dunn, *Adventures*, 225.

27. Dunn, *Adventures*, 215–216; Gibb, *Ibn Battuta: Travels*, 215–222.

28. For some other close calls, see Dunn, *Adventures*, 129–130, 155, 243–247; Gibb, *Ibn Battuta: Travels*, 261–265.

29. Boorstin, *The Discoverers*, 138; *Travels of Marco Polo*, xi; Joseph and Frances Gies, *Merchants and Moneymen: The Commercial Revolution, 1000–1500* (New York: Thomas Crowell, 1972), 130; Dunn, *Adventures*, 5.

Further Reading

ABERCROMBIE, THOMAS. "Ibn Battuta: Prince of Travelers," *National Geographic* (December 1991), 2–49. Compares how the lands Ibn Battuta visited have changed (or not changed) in six centuries.

DUNN, ROSS E. *The Adventures of Ibn Battuta: A Muslim Traveler of the 14th Century* (Berkeley: University of California Press, 1986). Best account of both the man and his times.

GIBB, H. A. R. *Ibn Battuta: Travels in Asia and Africa, 1325–1354* (London: George Rutledge and Sons, 1929). Edited, shorter version of the *Rihla*.

The Travels of Marco Polo, edited with an introduction by Milton Rugoff (New York: New American Library, 1961). Inexpensive and well-footnoted edition for nonscholars.

CHAPTER 9

Mansa Musa and Louis IX: Pilgrims and State Builders

How did the institution of monarchy differ in Europe and west Africa in the thirteenth and fourteenth centuries? In a religious age, does a king show he is powerful by being pious or does his piety help him become powerful?

It must have been a memorable sight. Imagine ninety camels loaded with gold, and 500 slaves marching before the king, each slave carrying a gold staff weighing four pounds. Such was the scene that July day in 1324 when Mansa Musa [*mansa* means "king" in the Mandingo language] of Mali, the most powerful west African state, emerged from the sands of the Sahara and entered Cairo, Egypt.

Mansa Musa (reigned 1307–1337) was a pilgrim, a Muslim making a *hadj*, or holy journey, to Mecca in Arabia (today Saudi Arabia), the birthplace of Muhammed.

Now imagine another occasion, three generations earlier, when a second foreign monarch is making his way toward that same Egyptian capital. King Louis IX of France (1214–1270) has just landed an army of European knights at the port of Damietta on the Egyptian coast. The sultan's troops have fled and the king has decided to march on Cairo. It is the summer of 1249, and he wishes to conquer Muslim Egypt as a prelude to "recapturing" the Christian holy places in Palestine.

King Louis IX was also a pilgrim, but his holy journey was a military one, one battle in a war in which men could gain grace and even heaven by conquering land for their God and by converting or destroying the infidel.

Louis of France, "the most Christian king," never reached his goal. Disease and rash action by some of his knights who got themselves trapped in the city of Mansourah prevented the king from conquering Egypt for the faith. Louis was captured by the Saracens, as the French called their opponents; he ransomed himself by returning the city of Damietta, and he finally returned to France in 1254. Mansa Musa, on the other hand, spent several months (and much gold) in Cairo before continuing to Mecca. He returned home the following year, a poorer but still powerful and pious ruler. Both of these men were remembered long after their deaths because of their holy journeys. France and the Sudanese kingdom of Mali were very different in political structure and culture during the thirteenth and fourteenth centuries. Yet the Muslim and pagan world of Mansa Musa and the Christian kingdom of Louis IX shared one characteristic: In both, religion was a powerful enough political force that a ruler could gain, keep, and demonstrate power through religious actions.

When he left for Mecca in 1324, Mansa Musa ruled over a kingdom that covered most of the western sudan.[1] Mali extended west from the Adrar des Ifores to the Atlantic just north of the mouth of the Senegal River and included much of the coast from that river south to what is now Ghana. Mansa Musa's kingdom was the largest of the three west African states that flourished between 700 and 1600 AD. Mali power was created primarily by Sundiata, Mansa Musa's great-uncle, during the first half of the thirteenth century—at the same time that Louis IX was consolidating his control over French barons prior to embarking on his first crusade. Within a century after Mansa Musa's death in 1337, the power of Mali would be eclipsed by that of its former tributary state, the Songhai empire.

Gold taken from the Bure area along the upper reaches of the Niger River formed the basis of Mali wealth. For centuries the people of the sudan had traded gold and slaves with the Muslim north African states across the Sahara. Since the black west Africans had long provided much of the precious metal that supported the commerce of the Muslim Mediterranean and west Asian countries, the gold that Mansa Musa took on his pilgrimage was notable only because of its quantity. Muslim merchants had long crisscrossed the Sahara with salt, iron, clothing, and spices which they traded for the gold and slaves of Ghana and Mali.

The Arab and Berber nomads from the north also brought their religion with them to the west African bazaars. Islam was a simple, monotheistic faith which preached submission to all-powerful Allah [Arabic term for God]. It was a religion attractive in its simplicity, with no priests or elaborate ritual. To pray daily, fast one month a year, and make a journey to Mecca once in your lifetime were central tenets of Islam. Perhaps more important in explaining why many west African rulers and traders turned to Islam is that Muslims from the north brought with them two skills essential to a trading people: writing and reckoning. Muslims did not send out missionaries explicitly to convert unbelievers as Christians did, and this may explain why Islam remained a "ruler cult" in Mali and other west African states. The majority of African peasants remained attached to their older nature religions. Only the upper classes in Mali were Muslim; they wished to be for personal and economic reasons, and they were not particularly troubled that the lower classes were not.[2] The Muslim traveling scholar Ibn Battuta, visiting Mali in 1352–1353 during the reign of Mansa Musa's brother Sulayman, found notable some of the "pagan" customs he observed at court. Petitioners humbled themselves before the king by covering themselves with dust; when the king commended one of his men, they sprinkled more dust on their heads and backs in appreciation. Ibn Battuta noticed that even the Islamic inhabitants of Mali often ate "animals not ritually slaughtered, and dogs and donkeys." Young women, "even the king's daughters," appeared naked in public.[3]

The un-Muslim behavior of persons at Mansa Musa's court is more understandable when we appreciate the nature of kingship in west African societies. Mali was not a territorial state of the modern sort; it was certainly not a nation, as we generally use that term. Mansa Musa's subjects were members of various status groups (noble, freeman, serf, slave) or occupational categories (hunter, fisherman, trader, farmer). These people were also members of various tribal or ethnic categories such as Soninke or Malinke which were themselves subdivided, often into groups of villages, each headed by a chief. The king of such an agglomeration of occupational, ethnic, and kinship groups was rather like the leader of a very large family, with each branch of the family or clan agreeing to provide the leader with tribute in the form of money, slaves, grain, or arms. Such allegiances were historically weaker and more temporary than they might have been if the king had been seen as the head of a fixed territory and, in some sense at least, the "owner" of the land, as was the case in France. Although west African kings, like European ones, had personal lands from which they drew an income, Mansa Musa had to hold his empire together by bonds of personal and family loyalty. This loyalty was based on how strong the "great man," or ruler, was, and on what he could do for his various peoples. The collection of taxes, as well as military service to the ruler, often depended upon how strong the king was perceived to be, not on his territorial or legal rights.

This system of west African kingship helps explain why Mansa Musa (and some of his predecessors in Mali) relied on fixed rituals at court and went on elaborate pilgrimages to Mecca. It was a way of showing strength and confidence, for only a strong ruler could command such public obedience and be absent from his kingdom for over a year. This display of strength would consolidate his rule at home upon his return and win him prestige in the wider Islamic community. That is what Mansa Musa hoped would happen, at any rate. To some extent, it seemed to work for him. It is not accidental that, on his way back from Mecca, he stopped in Gao to "receive the submission" of the Songhai ruler, one of his strongest potential enemies.

There is no doubt that this had impressed his Muslim brethren in the north. The king of Mali distributed so much gold during his visit to Cairo that the price of the metal was devalued by as much as twenty-five percent, according to some reports. Ten years after his visit, the natives of Egypt were still talking about their royal visitor. Mansa Musa distributed so much gold that he ran out of money before his return and was forced to borrow at excessive rates of interest (up to 175 percent). Such largess was neither foolishness nor merely an attempt to impress the foreigners, though he clearly did the latter. Providing handsomely for your retinue was a royal duty for an African king; supporting the poor and less fortunate was a religious duty for a Muslim. Mansa Musa was both a good ruler and a good Muslim.

Religious zeal helped motivate his actions and there is evidence that his pilgrimage strengthened his faith. Upon being told in Cairo that a Muslim should have only four wives, he asked if this also applied to kings. On being told that it did, he said, "By God, I did not know that. I renounce it [having more than four wives] from this moment."[4] The king of Mali returned home eager to strengthen education and purify Islam. He built new mosques, and ordered that Friday prayers and other basic tenets of Islam be more strictly observed. He promoted Islamic scholarship, and became a strong public advocate of the faith. This was both a pious and a wise move for, according to one historian, "in return for this support accorded to Islam by the king, the whole prestige of the . . . religion was directed to exhorting loyalty to the ruler."[5] Mansa Musa clearly used his religion as a state-building force. While we cannot know his innermost religious feelings, it is certainly true that having the Muslim *ulemas* [scholar-jurists] on his side would have strengthened the authority of this west African king.

A final characteristic of Mansa Musa was his concern for justice, a trait he shared with his European fellow pilgrim Louis IX. While it is true that gratitude for his promotion of Islam may have guided the pens of the Muslim travelers and historians, it is interesting, in light of later European views of "darkest Africa," that Ibn Battuta specifically mentioned the high standard of justice, order, and honesty that seemed to prevail in the Mali lands. All men and women, whether Muslim or not, whether black or white, were treated fairly. Theft was severely punished by death or enslavement, and there was order and prosperity in the emerging commercial centers of Niani, Timbuktu, and Gao. The city of Timbuktu, in particular, compared favorably in size, comfort, and general cultural level with many northern European cities during the fourteenth century.

The reign of Mansa Musa of Mali represents a high point in the history of traditional west African states. He brought the political kingship structure to a high level of development and graced his kingdom with an Islamic culture and ruling class. His near-contemporary Louis IX of France represents a similar peak in the development of medieval Christian kingship and state building. One standard historical reference work praises Louis of France, perhaps too grandly, as "the most chivalrous man of his age and the ideal medieval king. . . . His justice won him national support and made him the arbiter of Europe. His reign was the golden age of medieval France."[6] Louis may have been the greatest monarch of medieval France. If he is considered "ideal," however, it is precisely because he was able to combine effectively religious piety (he was canonized a saint in 1298) with practical political measures that strengthened the royal power in France. Like Mansa Musa, he was a good ruler and a pious one. Unlike the African ruler, Louis IX was almost the last French king to even pretend to saintliness. Louis may have been idealistic and chivalrous. If one characteristic of medieval life was taking religion very seriously, he most certainly was medieval.

Who else but a medieval Christian would go to Mass twice a day, recite extensive prayers daily, and receive Communion six times a year, approaching the altar each time on his knees? If we did not know better, we would think that this man who observed a strict fast during Lent, wore a hairshirt [a coarse, irritating haircloth undergarment worn as a form of penance for sins] to bed, and fed lepers with his own hands was a saintly hermit rather than a monarch. But a monarch he was. The man who hated foul language and heretics also nurtured a strong dislike for barons who disobeyed him. The king who endowed religious institutions throughout the kingdom and built the beautiful Gothic chapel of Sainte Chapelle to hold what was reputed to be a piece of the cross on which Christ was crucified also warned his son in his will to "take special care to have good bailiffs and provosts, and often to inquire of them . . . whether any of them are addicted to the vice of excessive covetousness, or untruthfulness or shifty behaviour."[7] His crusades against the infidel, launched against the advice of most of his counselors, were holy journeys that only a saintly monarch would wish to take and only a strong one could afford.

The great crusades of the twelfth century that had established European or "Latin" kingdoms in Palestine were long past when Louis decided to fulfill a vow and attack Egypt in the 1240s. Almost no one thought it wise to send 15,000 men in 1800 ships across the Mediterranean—no one but Louis, who was strong enough that no one could stop him. He had secured himself against his enemies at home for over a decade before he made the vow to "take the cross" [go on crusade wearing a garment prominently marked with a cross] in 1244.

Louis's mother, Blanche of Castile, who ruled for the young king until he was twenty, taught him the importance of keeping the royal power strong, and the ways to do this. Taking advantage of the rule of a woman, French noblemen under Raymond of Toulouse led a rebellion against the monarch from 1226 to 1231. When it was over, the lords of the provinces of Brittany and Boulogne had submitted and Blanche had arranged a marriage between the king and

Margaret of Provence that would bring that province into the French kingdom. In 1242 Louis held off an attack by the English king, Henry III, and some of the feudal lords in southern France. By the end of 1243 the provinces of Aquitaine and Toulouse were under royal control. Finally, in 1259, Louis signed a treaty with the English king, giving up the two small territories of Périgord and Limousin in return for the English renunciation of all claims to the much larger areas of Normandy, Maine, and Poitou.

While maintaining royal power against land-hungry counts and barons was a necessary prelude to any prolonged absence from the kingdom, it was also necessary that this royal government now being extended to new areas of France be operated efficiently and fairly. The image of the "good king Louis" enshrined in French legend was created in part by the story of the king sitting under an oak tree in Vincennes distributing justice to all who approached. This romantic tale, told by Louis's biographer Joinville, tends to obscure some of the king's more practical measures: establishing clear rights of appeal from local or baronial courts; appointing *enqueteurs* [royal investigators] to report to the king any injustices perpetrated by his regular officials; selecting men of the lesser nobility as lawyers and public servants since they would be more loyal to the king; and even staunchly refusing to allow churchmen to unduly influence his politics. Joinville is very clear on this last point. On one occasion the French bishops asked the king to insist that his subjects who had been excommunicated do penance and return to the good graces of the church. Louis said he would do this only if the bishops would let him review each case to determine if the excommunicates had been justly kicked out of the fold in the first place. When the bishops bridled at this royal interference in church affairs, he refused to help them. The fact that Louis could combine justice and Christian duty is nicely illustrated by another story from Joinville. Several times during the first of his crusades, Louis objected to his troops "consorting with prostitutes." On one occasion in Egypt he forced a knight arrested in a brothel to choose between being led bound with a rope through camp by a prostitute and giving up his horse and being dismissed from the army; the knight chose the latter.[8]

In the long run, of course, Louis IX is remembered more for his role in building the French royal state than for his two unsuccessful crusades, the second of which took his life in 1270. It is interesting that Louis himself regarded his faith, and the holy journeys he saw as a necessary result of that faith, as much more important than the measures he took to strengthen French royal justice. The office of *enqueteur*, for example, was originally established in the years immediately before the crusade of 1248–1254 so that these men could help him put the affairs of his land in order before he left for Egypt. Louis also rejected the opportunity to seize land from the English king in the 1250s because he was hoping to encourage Henry to join him in the next crusade. That crusade did not get beyond Tunis, where the king died. The crusading movement itself failed by 1291 when the last Christian stronghold in Palestine, the city of Acre, was retaken by the Muslims. Louis IX was intelligent enough to have foreseen the end; had he done so, and given up crusading on this account, he would have been less medieval. One can question whether he would have been more modern without his deep Christian faith, however, for the same faith that sent him on crusades convinced this king that he had to maintain "the rights of his subjects, the prerogatives of his crown, and the safety of his realm."[9]

Mansa Musa of Mali quite literally put his kingdom on the map. It was two years after his death in 1339 that Mali first appeared on a European map. Louis IX's medieval sense of justice and practical administrative skills helped make his kingdom one of the most powerful in Europe. Neither of these monarchs could or would have done what he did without the quality or quantity of faith that inspires pilgrimages. Neither Mansa Musa nor St. Louis was modern and yet each enjoyed careers and prerogatives that would be the envy of many modern heads of state. What modern leader would risk being out of touch with his people for two to four years at a time, as these men did? Mansa Musa and Louis IX could afford their journeys, even their mistakes, because in their world, kingship was sacred. If royalty had its privileges, so did divinity, and an aura of the divine surrounded medieval monarchs, both Muslim and Christian. The fact that this is no longer true is part of what makes us modern.

Notes

1. The word "sudan," used to describe the savanna lands that stretch across Africa south of the Sahara from coast to coast, is taken from an Arab word for "black."

2. J. S. Trimingham, *A History of Islam in West Africa* (Oxford: Oxford University Press, 1962), 37.
3. Said Hamdun and Noel King, editors, *Ibn Battuta in Black Africa* (London: Rex Collings, 1975), 39, 48.
4. Trimingham, *A History of Islam in West Africa*, 71.
5. Nehemiah Levtzion, *Ancient Ghana and Mali* (New York: Holmes and Meier, 1980), 193; J. S. Trimingham, *The Influence of Islam upon Africa*, Second Edition (London: Longmans Group Limited, 1980), 11.
6. William L. Langer, *New Illustrated Encyclopedia of World History*, Volume I (New York: Abrams, 1975), 250–251.
7. Jean de Joinville, "Life of St. Louis" in *Chronicles of the Crusades*, trans. by M. R. B. Shaw (Baltimore: Penguin Books, 1963), 349. Louis's Sainte Chapelle still stands in its original form, without fracture or reinforcement, after 700 years.
8. *Ibid.*, 177–178, 207, 292.
9. Margaret Wade Labarge, *St. Louis: Louis IX, Most Christian King of France* (Boston: Little, Brown, 1968), 249.

Further Reading

Chronicles of the Crusades, trans. by M. R. B. Shaw (Baltimore: Penguin Books, 1963). Good sample of medieval historical writing—and thinking.

LABARGE, MARGARET WADE. *St. Louis: Louis IX, Most Christian King of France* (Boston: Little, Brown, 1968). Readable biography.

LEVTZION, NEHEMIAH. *Ancient Ghana and Mali* (New York: Holmes and Meier, 1980). Clear, short, factual account, one of the few available.

TRIMINGHAM, J. S. *A History of Islam in West Africa* (Oxford: Oxford University Press, 1962). Good source for study of Islam south of the Sahara.

CHAPTER 10

Prince Henry and Zheng He: Sailing South

How do the structures and values of a society affect the way people view economic and political expansion and contact with other cultures?

It somehow doesn't seem fair. Prince Henry of Portugal (1394–1460), who was land-bound, is known to history as Henry the Navigator while the Chinese admiral Zheng He (ca. 1371–1435), who commanded fleets with hundreds of ships, is remembered as a eunuch, if at all. Of course, Henry's personal ability to navigate—if he had any—is not what made his life significant. Zheng He's condition as a eunuch [castrated male] did not affect his ability to lead men or manage fleets. Each man is remembered as he is because of the conditions and values of his society. These conditions and values also helped to determine how the Chinese and Portuguese reacted to the voyages of their remarkable explorers.

Between 1405 and 1433, the emperors of the Ming dynasty (1368–1644) created a fleet and ordered it to make seven expeditions into the "Great Western Sea," or Indian Ocean. The man selected to command these voyages, the most ambitious in Chinese history, was born Ma He, a member of a Muslim family of Mongol descent in the province of Yunnan. When the first Ming emperor incorporated this Mongol province into his empire in 1381, Ma He was captured, castrated, and taken to the imperial capital of Nanjing, probably to serve as a harem guard. At age twenty, Ma He entered the service of the royal prince Zhu Di and very soon distinguished himself as a junior officer in a civil war that brought a new emperor to power. In 1404 the new emperor, Yongle (reigned

1403–1424), promoted Ma He to the position of superintendent of the office of eunuchs and honored him with the Chinese surname Zheng. At about this time, the new head eunuch was described as tall and handsome, a man who "walks like a tiger and talks in a commanding voice."[1]

It was this commanding figure whom the emperor chose as leader of his new fleet. In this role, Zheng He's task proved enormous; he was to undertake seven voyages, each of which lasted nearly two years. On his first voyage in 1405–1407, he commanded 28,000 men on 317 ships, many of them large "treasure ships" 440 feet long and 180 feet wide. By contrast, Columbus "discovered" America eighty-five years later with 120 men and a fleet of three ships, one of which was seventy-five feet long. Zheng He's first expedition traveled to India, with stops at Java and Ceylon. The fourth expedition in 1413–1415 reached Aden and Hormuz on the Persian Gulf, and on the seventh expedition in 1431–1433 the Chinese sent a small group to visit Mecca; they also touched the east coast of Africa as far south as Malindi near the modern state of Kenya. At each stop, Zheng He presented lavish gifts to the local rulers from "their" emperor and recorded information about interesting customs and creatures he encountered. *Overall Survey of the Ocean's Shores Annotated* was written by Zheng He's fellow Muslim Ma Huan; it was based on a diary that Ma Huan kept during the third, fifth, and seventh voyages.[2] Ma Huan's book shows the great interest the Chinese took in the dress, food, language, marriage and death rituals, and flora and fauna of the countries they visited. According to most modern historians of China, however, anthropological research was not the primary purpose of these costly trips.

There were a number of reasons why the court of the Son of Heaven initiated these voyages, discounting for the moment the exuberance of a young ruler and a natural curiosity about his neighbors to the south and west. To consolidate his power won in a civil war, the emperor decided to send what the Chinese called tribute missions to all neighboring countries to set up diplomatic exchanges. Owing to their advanced civilization, the Chinese, like other people before and since, believed that all other cultures were inferior and that once foreigners became familiar with Chinese culture they would realize it was the source of all wisdom and political power. While some representatives of foreign states felt the Chinese claim was unwarranted, many kowtowed [bowed] before the emperor either because they regarded it as appropriate, or because it enabled them to establish trade relations with the Chinese. Zheng He's voyages, then, were part of the Yongle emperor's effort to strengthen his own power by strengthening and expanding the tribute system. The voyages were also designed in part to curb Japanese piracy along the eastern coast of China, to check on possible Mongol activity in western Asia, and to search for treasure and overawe a few "barbarians." Zheng He accomplished these aims in visits to at least thirty-seven countries, many more than once. At the end of his fourth voyage in 1415, he brought back the envoys of thirty states to do homage to the Chinese emperor.[3] He also brought back a giraffe and a zebra to astonish the court; this latter creature, whose Swahili name sounded similar to the Chinese word for unicorn, was celebrated at court as a good omen for the dynasty and as an "emblem of Perfect Virtue, Perfect Government and Perfect Harmony in the Empire and in the Universe."[4] Zheng He's work had clearly boosted Ming prestige as well as increased Chinese trade with south and west Asia.

Therefore, from a Western perspective, it is surprising that the voyages of Zheng He were abruptly halted in 1433 and never resumed. Zheng He himself died several years after his last voyage. The exact date of his death, like that of his birth, is uncertain. After this, the Chinese went back to fighting nomads on the northern land frontier, something they had done for centuries. Japanese pirates soon reappeared along the southern coast. Zheng He's name lived on as the name of a Buddhist temple in Thailand and as the name of a well in Malacca.[5] In China, however, Zheng He and his travels to the "Western Ocean" were soon forgotten. A generation after his last voyage, an official in the Ministry of Defense even burned the logbooks of the expedition, whether deliberately or by accident, whether at the command of the emperor or on his own, no one seems to know.

We do know that a far different fate awaited the work of Prince Henry of Portugal, a man who became a legend in European history. Born in 1394 as the third son of King John I and Queen Philippa of Portugal, Henry became famous as the man whose sailors explored the west coast of Africa during the first half of the fifteenth century. Every grade school student knows that without the pioneering explorations of Prince Henry the Navigator, Bartholomew Dias would not have been able to round the Cape of Good Hope in

1487–1488, Vasco da Gama would not have sailed to India and back in 1497–1499, and Columbus would not have sought a sea route to the Indies in 1492.

Although he never personally navigated any ships south, Henry did make it his life's work to send out ship after ship from his rocky outpost of Sagres on the Atlantic coast of Portugal. Henry either outfitted the ships himself or granted a license to private captains who would repay him with a fifth of everything valuable they brought back. In the early years, when his ships were hugging the African desert lands, Henry usually spent far more than he earned. Although his ships were much smaller than those of Zheng He, Henry's record was impressive for his time and place. Men working under his direction settled in the Madeiras and discovered and settled the Azores and some of the Cape Verde Islands. In 1434, Gil Eanes finally sailed beyond Cape Bojador on the west coast of Africa after Portuguese sailors had refused or been unable to do so on fourteen earlier trips. Many men feared sailing too far south. Current rumors included the belief that anyone passing Cape Bojador would turn black, that the sea boiled in the tropics, and that the sun's rays descended in the form of liquid fire as you approached the equator. Once the Portuguese passed Cape Bojador, a barrier more psychological than physical had been breached.

The Portuguese caravels [light, fast, maneuverable ships that could be sailed inshore] continued their journeys south in the late 1430s and 1440s. Alfonzo Goncalves Baldaia went 300 miles beyond Bojador in 1435, and in 1441 Nuno Tristao went down as far as Cape Blanco, halfway between Sagres and the equator. It was in this decade that Cape Verde was rounded, although it was not until the year of Prince Henry's death, in 1460, that Pedro de Sintra reached Sierra Leone. In the early years, Henry constantly had to urge his sailors "to go back and go further." It was easier and more profitable to pirate Muslim vessels in the north than it was to take the more fearful route southwest along the barren desert coast. However, after several blacks were brought back to Portugal as slaves in 1441, the number and willingness of Henry's sailors grew. The slave trade and African exploration became intertwined, and Henry built the first European trading post used for slaves on Arguin Island in 1448.

While Prince Henry did not set out to secure slaves, the new trade in human beings did not trouble him greatly. Slaves had souls that could be saved and that appealed to Henry as much as did the selling and civilizing of them. Unlike his Chinese counterpart, whose voyages had no religious aims at all, Henry had a strong desire to spread his faith and fight the infidel Moors [Muslims in northwest Africa]. Zheng He, a Muslim, made no attempt to offend the religiosity of those he encountered. Personally, he offered sacrifices to a Chinese sea goddess before each voyage, but on a tablet he placed in Ceylon in 1409 with inscriptions in Chinese, Persian, and Tamil, he offered thanks to Buddha, Allah, and the Hindu god Vishnu—all of whom were worshipped on that island. Writing such an "ecumenical" inscription would have been literally unthinkable to Henry of Portugal. Indeed, his early interest in west African exploration was stimulated by the Portuguese conquest of the Muslim city of Ceuta on the north African coast in 1415; in 1437 Henry and his brother Fernando unsuccessfully attacked the city of Tangier, near Ceuta in Muslim Morocco.

The word "crusader" has medieval associations that contrast with our image of Henry as one of the first modern explorers, but the objectives of Henry the Navigator make him a crusader in the typical Iberian fashion. A major objective of his African expeditions was to "get behind" or outflank the Moors by sea. Like other medieval Christians, he had heard about the legendary Prester John, a Christian king in Africa somewhere south of the Sahara. If the Portuguese could reach Guinea, as they called black western Africa, they might be able to find an ally who could attack the infidel Muslims from the south. His desire to secure military allies contrasts sharply with Zheng He, who sought only tribute, information, and the opportunity to present gifts.

Although his explorations failed to secure Henry's military or diplomatic objectives against the Moors, they provided new geographical knowledge that improved future mapmaking and encouraged further Portuguese exploration. They also allowed him to promote trade and increase Portugal's political power at Spain's expense by controlling many Atlantic islands. In sum, Henry the Navigator's program mixed religion with politics in a way designed to appeal to the various components of Portuguese society. His brother, King Duarte I, supported Henry's work by granting him several royal monopolies. These gave him a fifth of everything of value brought back from south of Cape Bojador and made him the "landlord" of the Madeiras, the Azores, and Cape Verde. Henry also held the monopoly on all fishing and coral gathering along the Atlantic and Mediterranean coasts of Portugal and received all fees paid by fishermen to fish in these areas. He was reputed to be the "richest man in Portugal" after the king, but he probably died in debt because of the money he spent on exploration. The Portuguese merchants supported Henry's work because of the potential profits to be gained from exploration and the slave trade. Even Portuguese pirates were pleased by the opportunity his work gave them to raid and plunder under the cover of "exploring." The Catholic Church supported Henry's missionary efforts to convert the heathen and fight the infidel, and the aristocracy generally liked both the idea of crusading and the idea of increasing Portuguese power. The loyal peasants, we must assume, enjoyed Portuguese greatness vicariously, as most peasants in most places enjoy most forms of greatness.

Because of the broad-based support for Henry's work that existed within Portuguese society, he did not need to be a navigator. One modern historian, critical of the myth of Henry as a nautical genius who ran a "school" for geographers and sailors at Sagres, put the matter quite simply: "Henry harnessed his own talents and energies to those of his family and country. He did not need to invent ships, train sailors, educate pilots or give courage to his men. He found all these at his command. What he needed to do, and what he did, was to give focus to Portuguese energies."[6]

It was perhaps this as much as anything—the energies already there—that made the voyages organized by Prince Henry of Portugal the start of the "age of discovery and exploration" that we read about in our texts, while those of Zheng He, the Ming admiral, remained "mere exploits."[7] We should not forget the interesting similarities between Henry and Zheng He. Both sought power for their respective rulers, though in different ways. While neither favored outright conquest of the lands he explored, both found the idea of economic domination by the "mother country" acceptable. Both had sailing vessels suitable for long ocean voyages. Yet Henry's voyages marked a beginning and those of Zheng He an ending of maritime activity. Why?

One reason this question is so intriguing is that we have the benefit of hindsight. We know what came of the voyages of Prince Henry. We know how, in the words of one of his biographers, "he set a nation's steps upon a path that led to the world's end."[8] And we know as well what happened to China—and we wonder what might have happened. With their larger vessels and technical superiority (Chinese sailors had the magnetic compass in the eleventh century, perhaps two centuries before their European counterparts), would it have been that difficult for the Chinese to have dominated all of southeast Asia and established their power in India and even portions of Africa?[9] There was already a substantial overseas Chinese population in southeast Asia, and it showed every prospect of growing when the voyages were ended. If the Chinese had followed up on the voyages of Zheng He, what would the world be like today? They did not do this, of course. Instead China began to suffer from the intrusions of European sailors as early as the sixteenth century, just a century after Zheng He's voyages. China became prey to the West by 1850; it might have been Europe's strongest competitor. So much for speculation. What is certain is that the very structure of Chinese society in the fifteenth century made it difficult for Zheng He to be the pioneer that Henry was, even assuming that he wanted to be such a pioneer. Zheng He was a skilled administrator, diplomat, and seaman, but he was, above all, a servant of his emperor. His advancement in society depended on the emperor, not on any skills he might possess. There was little place in Ming society for a private or independent entrepreneur [risk-taking capitalist]. Trade was a government monopoly. The Son of Heaven employed servants such as Zheng He to do his will; he would never "contract out" exploration as the Portuguese king did.

There were also clear anticommercial and antiforeign biases in Chinese society during this time. The government got its money from taxes on land, not from taxing private traders and merchants. In addition, farming was considered more virtuous than business (as it was in medieval Europe until about this same time). Both Confucian and Christian ideologies glorified those who worked the land over those who soiled their hands with money. In the West, however, the diversity of states and their competition with each other as well as the perceived need for outside goods "from the East" stimulated the rise of capitalist towns and trade after 1150. The crusades of this century also helped break down traditional biases against commerce in Europe. China was more self-sufficient and thus faced no real pressure to change the traditional attitude toward either trade or outsiders.[10] The inhabitants of the Middle Kingdom (Ma Huan's translator calls it "the Central Country") did not look down upon outsiders because they were genetically programmed to do so; they did it because they could afford to: Their country was more prosperous than neighboring ones in the fifteenth century.

Given this, it is logical that the Chinese would simply view sea power as less important than maintaining a strong land army. It was. The chief threat to fifteenth-century China came from the northern barbarians; they, not Japanese pirates, were to overrun the country in the seventeenth century. All this means that both the Chinese and the Portuguese were quite sensible in choosing the course of action they did. There is nothing in the records, meager as they are, to suggest that Zheng He himself dreamed of a Chinese maritime empire. He may have, just as Henry may have wondered once or twice whether sailing down the coast of Africa would really defeat the Moors. Neither of these men of action spent much time pondering the consequences of his actions for future generations. That pondering they leave to us.

Notes

1. B. Martin and S. Chien-lung, "Cheng Ho: Explorer and Navigator," in *Makers of China: Confucius to Mao* (New York: Halstead Press, 1972), 112. Cheng, although his surname, is placed first in Chinese. [The spelling Zheng He used in this chapter represents the new Pinyin system of transliteration adopted by scholars only in recent years.]
2. Ma Huan, *Overall Survey of the Ocean's Shores Annotated*, edited and introduced by J. V. G. Mills (Cambridge: Cambridge University Press, 1970).
3. Jung-pang Lo, "Cheng Ho," in *Encyclopaedia Britannica*, 15th edition, *Macropedia*, Volume 4 (Chicago: Macmillan, 1974), 193–194.
4. Nora C. Buckley, "The Extraordinary Voyages of Admiral Cheng Ho," *History Today* (July 1975), 468.
5. Ma Huan, *Overall Survey of the Ocean's Shores*, editor's introduction, 7.
6. Bailey W. Diffie and George D. Winius, *Foundations of the Portuguese Empire 1415–1580* (Minneapolis: University of Minnesota Press, 1977), 122.
7. Ma Huan, *Overall Survey of the Ocean's Shores*, editor's introduction, 34.
8. Elaine Sanceau, *Henry the Navigator: The Story of a Great Prince and His Times* (New York: W. W. Norton, 1947), 247.
9. Fernand Braudel, *Capitalism and Material Life, 1400–1800* (New York: Harper, 1973), 308, says that a Japanese junk, constructed much like those of Zheng He, traveled from Japan to Acapulco in 1610.
10. See Lynda Schaffer, "China, Technology, and Change," *World History Bulletin*, Volume IV (Fall, Winter 1986–1987), 1, 4–6; Paul Kennedy, *The*

Rise and Fall of the Great Powers: Economic Change and Military Conflict from 1500–2000 (New York: Random House, 1987), 8, notes that members of the Confucian ruling class (mandarins) distrusted merchants because they had less control over them. The mandarins hindered foreign trade by confiscating the property of merchants or banning their businesses on occasion.

Further Reading

BUCKLEY, NORA C. "The Extraordinary Voyages of Admiral Cheng Ho," *History Today* (July 1975), 464–469.

MA HUAN. *Overall Survey of the Ocean's Shores Annotated*, edited and introduced by J. V. G. Mills (Cambridge: Cambridge University Press, 1970). Exciting look at what fifteenth-century Chinese thought important.

SANCEAU, ELAINE. *Henry the Navigator: The Story of a Great Prince and His Times* (New York: W. W. Norton, 1947). Flowery hero worship in places but still useful and interesting reading.

CHAPTER 11

Erasmus and Luther: The Reformer's Dilemma

To what extent is it possible to reform an institution from within? What intellectual and personal qualities cause some individuals to be more radical than others, and what are the implications of such choices in history?

During the last two centuries of the European Middle Ages (1300–1500) people took religion more seriously than most of us can imagine. Bestselling books of the day "gave instructions, not on how to pay income tax, but on how to escape Hell."[1] This world, into which Desiderius Erasmus (1466–1536) and Martin Luther (1483–1546) were born, was one in which both heaven and hell seemed much closer to people than they do today. One reason was that life was shorter and more precarious for most people than it is for us.

Men and women heard stories of the Black Death, a plague which had carried off one-third of the population in many parts of Europe in 1348–1349, and which occasionally reappeared. They also experienced wars and famines that periodically swept through the countryside. Persons in the upper classes knew that princes and merchants gained and lost fortunes during these years as men fought to get their share of the new wealth coming from the East.

The Christian church, too, had to respond to this change and uncertainty. No longer as politically powerful as it had been in the thirteenth century, the church could no longer dominate kings and princes as it once had. And it could do little to control the plague or the economy. It could, however, take advantage of the longing for certainty of salvation which possessed many people in the days when Erasmus and Luther were growing up.

119

While Christian leaders found it difficult to explain why God had sent disease to bedevil men and women, they continued to comfort people with various forms of external piety to make them feel closer to God as they faced death from plagues, wars, or famines. Medieval Christians could assure themselves of God's favor (grace) and keep themselves in a "state of grace" (the opposite of a "state of sin") by undertaking any number of good actions, most of which cost time, money, or both. Clergymen encouraged the faithful to go on pilgrimages to holy places, usually shrines of saints, like that of Thomas Becket in Canterbury. Some princes and bishops also collected relics, usually portions of the bones or clothing of saintly individuals, which they were willing to allow people to view for a price. People could also pay a priest to say Masses for the salvation of their souls. Finally, one could receive an "indulgence," the remission of punishment for past sins, in exchange for specified prayers and/or an offering of money to support a good cause. Indulgences could help a person escape all punishment for sins (in purgatory) and go straight to heaven after he or she died.

All these good works gave some comfort to those desperate for tangible evidence of earned "grace." They also helped enrich the institutional church which had control of their distribution. This "good works" theology, and the political power of the institutional church which lay behind it, offended the spiritual sensitivities of men like Erasmus and Luther who saw Christianity as a matter of inner devotion to Christ, and not primarily a matter of good works. These men, along with others, regarded the church as sorely in need of reform.

And it was reform of the church which they accomplished, though hardly in the way either preferred or imagined. Martin Luther sparked the famous sixteenth-century Reformation in 1517 when he wrote his famous list of "ninety-five theses" explaining errors in the church's policy on indulgences as preached by the German Dominican priest Johan Tetzel. In this statement, Luther asserted that God's free grace and not human works was responsible for our salvation. Luther was influenced by others, among them Desiderius Erasmus, a Christian humanist who suggested that true religion was much simpler and more Scriptural than the official church seemed to believe. After 1516, Luther prepared his university lectures and sermons using a copy of the Greek New Testament edited by Erasmus, whom he admired. After the Reformation began to divide most of Europe politically and religiously by the mid-1520s, it was said that "Erasmus laid the egg that Luther hatched," that Luther was merely taking to their logical conclusion some of the ideas of Erasmus. Erasmus denied this and, despite his early defense of Luther and his ideas, refused to reject the Roman church. Luther, by contrast, was excommunicated by the pope in 1520 and, in an act of public defiance, burned the letter of excommunication.

Both Erasmus and Luther were men who wished to improve the institutional church and the spiritual lives of its members. Their disagreements with each other—Erasmus deplored Luther's "violence" and the "tragedy" of a divided Christendom, while Luther denounced Erasmus as a coward and pagan who did not *really* understand Scripture after all—highlight the reformer's dilemma. Is it better to seek change from within an institution, even if you are likely to get less change that way? Or is it better to act boldly and accept the risk of getting expelled, as Luther was willing to do by 1520, in order to preserve your integrity and the opportunity to make more significant reforms? Is it better to promote greater change for fewer people, or less change for more people? Luther chose the first option; Erasmus the second. Their personal histories help explain their decisions.

By his own account, Erasmus of Rotterdam was born the bastard child of a priest on October 27, 1466.[2] Despite the circumstances of his birth, his parents cared for him well until their death from the plague when he was about fourteen. During his early years, Erasmus received a humanistic education at a monastic school in the Netherlands which stressed inward spirituality and devotion to Christ more than doctrine or dogma. This emphasis would remain a part of Erasmus's "Christian philosophy" throughout his life.[3]

Erasmus entered an Augustinian monastery at Steyn in 1487. Later he claimed he was ill with fever at the time and was "duped" into believing he could seriously pursue scholarship in the monastery. Erasmus took the religious vows of poverty, chastity, and obedience and was ordained a priest in 1492. He took the first opportunity, however, to leave the monastery, worked as secretary to the bishop of Cambrai for several years, and in 1495 began work on a doctor's degree in theology at the University of Paris.[4] While in Paris, Erasmus found, as Luther did later, that he disliked the irrelevant "how-many-angels-can-sit-on-the-head-of-a-pin" sort of questions that preoccupied many medieval theologians. He did find himself attracted to the study of the ancient Greek and Roman virtues which occupied the attention of a group of men known as humanists. These scholars were involved in the intellectual movement known as the Renaissance and its revival of interest in classical learning, beginning in Italy about 1300 and spreading north during the next three centuries. During his student years in Paris and a visit in 1499 to England, where he met the famous Renaissance humanists John Colet and Thomas More, Erasmus evolved a synthesis of classical virtue and Christian piety which he felt could be used to reform the lives of individual Christians and thereby the church itself. From such pagan authors as Cicero he took the virtues of *humanitas* [love of mankind based on a belief in the dignity of man as a rational creature] and *concordia* [a rational harmonizing of conflicting viewpoints]. From Christian writers such as Jerome and from Scripture, Erasmus took the virtues of compassion, patience, forgiveness, humility, and love.[5]

Armed with his new convictions about the relationship between holiness and "good letters" or scholarship, Erasmus began to promote his beliefs. In an early work, *The Handbook of the Christian Soldier*, written in 1501, Erasmus argued that accurate knowledge of Scripture was extremely important to a Christian, and that religion was primarily a matter of inward devotions, love of God, and love of neighbor. In his witty, direct, but abrasive style, Erasmus wrote:

> You venerate saints; you are glad to touch their relics. But you condemn what good they have left, namely the example of a pure life. . . . You wish to deserve well of Peter and Paul? Imitate the faith of one, the charity of the other—and you will . . . do more than if you were to dash back and forth to Rome ten times. . . .[6]

To make the new learning possible for more Christians, Erasmus spent several years learning Greek so he could construct an improved edition of the New Testament from available manuscripts. This work, published in 1516, included a preface in which he wrote enthusiastically about his hope that someday God's word would be available to all. Christ's teachings were simple enough, he believed, that all men and women should have access to them in their own languages. "We embellish a wooden or stone statue with gems and gold for the love of Christ. Why not, rather, mark with gold and gems . . . these writings which bring Christ to us so much more effectively than any paltry image?"[7]

While some considered these judgments of Erasmus, by now a famous scholar, irreverent and perhaps even heretical, his attacks on the misuse of power by church leaders, their exaggeration of the trivial, and their ignorance were continuous and very deliberate. In his commentary on the New Testament, he would occasionally stretch a point to make the text apply "to the familiar targets of his criticism, the corruption of the clergy, the ignorance of the theologians . . . empty ceremonies, vows, penance, relics, and monasticism." Perhaps even more subversive was a satire which Erasmus wrote anonymously in 1513, *Julius Exclusus*. In this work, the warrior-pope Julius II is excluded from heaven by St. Peter because, instead of teaching "true doctrine," he has made the church "splendid with regal palaces, splendid horses and mules, troops of servants, armies, officers . . . glamorous prostitutes and obsequious pimps."[8]

Given the tone of many of Erasmus's criticisms of the church, it is not surprising that people would expect the Dutch humanist to be an early and enthusiastic supporter of the German reformer Martin Luther, since Luther and Erasmus criticized many of the same abuses. Such was not the case. From the beginning, Erasmus's support of Luther was hesitant and qualified; it soon turned to bitter disappointment. To understand why this happened we must understand that Luther's attack on the church came from a theological rather than a humanistic direction. "Erasmus was concerned about ignorance, Luther about sin," one author wrote.[9] The fact that Luther changed forever the religious map of Europe shows which of the two concerns most sixteenth-century believers took more seriously.

Not only sin, but life itself, was serious for the Saxon mining family into which Luther was born in 1483. His parents were strict and his early religious training a mixture of traditional piety and half-pagan beliefs in gnomes, fairies, sprites, and witches.[10] Like Erasmus, Luther had a sensitive soul, but grew up in a far less cosmopolitan environment. Perhaps it was to be expected that the young Luther, despite acquiring great learning in his later life, would spend many years seeking to be certain he was worthy of salvation.

For over fifteen years, Martin Luther sought that certainty of salvation by living as an Augustinian monk, a priest, and a teacher in the Saxon towns of Erfurt and Wittenberg. Luther was bright and energetic as well as earnest; he advanced far more rapidly than most after entering the cloister [monastic house] in Erfurt in the summer of 1505. Two years later he was ordained a priest, and five years after that, in 1512, he was made a doctor of theology, an honor usually given only those in their forties or older. By this time, Luther was professor of bible at the University of Wittenberg. One of his regular responsibilities was to preach and lecture to his colleagues in the cloister as well as to students. While preparing lectures on the Psalms and Paul's Epistle to the Romans, Luther experienced his great insight about faith.

Since he took his faith very seriously, Luther had been troubled for years by the feeling that no matter how hard he tried, no matter how carefully he performed his religious duties or confessed his sins, God remained angry at him. Luther struggled during these years to accept the fact that God did indeed love him. Sometime between 1512 and 1517, Luther had a "conversion experience." While reading Paul's words in the Epistle to the Romans, "the righteous shall live by faith," Luther became convinced that nothing men or women can do can earn them salvation. People are saved by "faith alone" and not by any good or pious works.[11] This would become a central insight of the Protestant Reformation.

It was this basic insight, and the trust in Scripture which made it credible for him, that gave Luther courage to walk the road to Reformation. The first step on this road was the 1517 writing of the theses against doctrinal errors associated with the practice of granting indulgences. Though hindsight calls this the beginning of the Reformation, it was not immediately dramatic. More important were the events of the next four years: his debate with the theologian Johann Eck in 1519 in Leipzig, in which he denied the authority of the pope when it conflicted with Scripture; the pope's excommunication of him in 1520; and the meeting of the German princes at Worms in 1521, at which time he refused to deny his teachings and was declared an outlaw.

In addition, during the year 1520, Luther wrote three essays which, taken together, defined the major principles of Protestant or Reformed Christianity. In his *Address to the German Nobility*, Luther challenged the authority of the Roman pope in particular and the status of the clergy in general; he declared his belief in the priesthood of all believers. In *The Babylonian Captivity of the Church*, he attacked the sacraments as, for the most part, good works unjustified in Scripture. Eventually Luther and the Protestants reduced the sacraments to two, Baptism and Eucharist (Communion). Finally, in *The Freedom of the Christian*, Luther expressed his belief in salvation by faith. When the elector of Saxony, Luther's prince, decided to protect him against the agents of the German emperor in 1521, it became clear that this theological rift had political overtones which might make it far less easy to heal than was apparent in 1517.

Back in Louvain (today in Belgium but then in the Netherlands) Erasmus was beginning to worry. He understood from the beginning of Luther's attack on indulgences that the German friar shared his dislike of external piety. Erasmus, however, disliked Luther's wholesale attack on church authority and his often strident language. (Luther called the Roman pope the "whore of Babylon" and the Antichrist.) In a letter to Luther in May 1519, Erasmus suggested that "more can be accomplished by polite restraint than by vehemence." He also believed that "it is more advisable to scream out against those who abuse papal authority than against the popes themselves." To a mutual friend, however, Erasmus expressed his general support of Luther. "I pray," he wrote in July 1520, "that the supreme and wonderful Christ will so temper Luther's pen that he can be of very great profit to evangelical piety. . . . [Among] Luther's opponents I see many men who breathe the spirit of the world rather than of Christ."[12]

Erasmus's qualified support for Luther from 1519 to 1521 was based on their shared dislike of abuses and on the behavior of Luther's enemies. Rather than trying to prove Luther wrong from Scripture, as he challenged them to do, the Roman officials used authority: You cannot possibly be right because we have power and tradition on our side; if you do not recant, we will excommunicate you; we are not interested in the reasons for your position, just in whether or not you will stubbornly persist in holding to it. Writing to one of Luther's enemies, the archbishop of Mainz, in 1519, Erasmus said that "if [Luther] is innocent, I do not want him crushed by a faction of rogues, and if he is in error, I wish him to be corrected, not destroyed. This approach agrees better with the example of Christ." A year later, in November 1520, Erasmus met with Luther's prince, Frederick of Saxony, in Cologne. Frederick had asked for Erasmus's advice on the Luther question prior to the meeting with the emperor (Diet of Worms) to be held the following spring. Erasmus wrote a list of statements or axioms as guidance for Frederick. They suggested that the attack on Luther was caused "by the hatred of letters" and the "desire for supremacy." Erasmus added that those "closest to the Gospel teaching are said to be the least offended by Luther"; he noted that "this affair" should "be settled by the mature deliberation of serious and impartial men."[13]

But this would not happen. The papal letter condemning Luther was so violent that both Luther and Erasmus questioned whether it really came from the pope. It had. The declaration of the Diet of Worms making Luther an outlaw soon divided the German princes into two camps. Even in his 1520 axioms for Frederick, Erasmus had written prophetically: "The case is tending toward a greater crisis than certain men suppose." In succeeding years he continued to lament the "dangerous dissension" and the "tragedy" of the Luther affair. Several times he referred to the "bitter medicine" of Luther which, if swallowed, might produce good health in the church.[14]

For Erasmus the tragedy rapidly became a personal one. He was caught in the middle, with both sides insistently urging him to speak out on their behalf. For several years he continued to write critically about abuses in the church but refused to "join" the reformers in Germany or elsewhere because he believed one could correct abuses without leaving the Roman church. One did not have to attack papal authority, for example, in order to reform one's personal religious life in accord with the dictates of Scripture. Finally, in 1524, Erasmus did attack Luther's belief that man's will was so corrupted that without grace he could not do anything meritorious. To Erasmus's *Diatribe on the Freedom of the Will*, Luther responded in 1525 with his *On the Enslaved Will*. Although both men "talked past one another" in this debate, with each guilty of misunderstanding or exaggerating the views of the other, the exchange does illustrate the fundamental differences between the two reformers. Luther, in one of his extravagant and violent moods when he responded to the Dutch humanist, called him "a babbler, a skeptic, an Epicurean hog—stupid, hypocritical, and ignorant of Scripture."[15] There were clear temperamental differences separating these two reformers. Erasmus was a quiet scholar who could see nothing to be gained by shouting. Twice during these years, he changed residences when the political temperature got too hot. He left Louvain for Basel, Switzerland, in 1521 because of the anti-Luther sentiment in Louvain. The tumult of the Reformation in Basel drove him from that city in 1529 for five years. "I have seriously and openly discouraged violence," Erasmus wrote in 1524 to his friend and Luther's close associate Philip Melanchthon. "Even if I were an ardent devotee of the papist faction, I would still oppose violence, because that path only leads to more violence."[16] He was right, and there is nothing in his life to suggest he was not absolutely sincere on this point.

Yet there were also more than temperamental differences separating Erasmus and Luther—and these Erasmus did not fully understand. As early as 1517, after receiving Erasmus's New Testament translation, Luther wrote to a colleague that he was suspicious of Erasmus's love of pagan learning. "I am afraid . . . that he does not advance the cause of Christ and grace of God sufficiently," Luther wrote. This feeling that Erasmus somehow put knowledge above grace continued to bother Luther in later years and shows up clearly in the debate on free will.[17] Luther correctly saw the differences between himself and Erasmus as theological. In the words of Roland Bainton, the biographer of both men, they simply had different concepts of salvation: "This for Luther consisted in the forgiveness of sins by a sheer act of God's grace, for Erasmus in fellowship with God calling for a human response."[18]

Given this difference, all of Erasmus's talk about Luther's enemies really being enemies of "good learning," a theme that runs through Erasmus's letters, is beside the point. So too is Erasmus's belief that if only Luther and the Papists would lower their voices and talk reasonably about the self-evident truth of Scripture, the differences could be ironed out. Luther could not have done this, even if he had been a calmer person less given to abusive language. His God was simply not the one Erasmus worshipped. His God was a demanding one, not interested in the rational moderation stressed by many humanists. In the words of Bainton again, "The God of Luther, as of Moses, was the God who inhabits the storm clouds and rides on the wings of the wind. At his nod the earth trembles, and the people before him are as a drop in the bucket. He is a God of majesty and power. . . ."[19]

It is ironic that despite his differences with Erasmus, his strong language, and his clear resentment of Roman abuses, Luther did not see himself as a German nationalist and did not really want to divide the church. He called for "repentance and renewal" and was like Erasmus in simply wanting people to live virtuous lives based on Scripture.[20]

Yet the work of Martin Luther and, after him, John Calvin and others did bring about major changes in the Christian church. The Catholic bishops at the Council of Trent (1545–1563) reasserted their basic doctrines and made no attempt to accommodate the ideas of the reformers. Before long, Western Christendom was fragmented into hundreds of denominations and sects. Attempts to restore unity in dozens of bloody religious wars failed as Catholics and Protestants rejected the muted calls for a measure of mutual tolerance. It was common in that day to prove your love of God by hatred of your "heretic" or "papist" neighbor. It is only in our own day, a more ecumenical one, that some people have begun to better understand the real aims of both Erasmus and Luther and ask: "What if . . . ?"

Notes

1. Roland H. Bainton, *Here I Stand: A Life of Martin Luther* (Nashville: Abingdon Press, 1950), 29.
2. Desiderius Erasmus, *Christian Humanism and the Reformation: Selected Writings*, edited by John C. Olin (New York: Harper and Row, 1965), 23–25.
3. *Ibid.*; Roland H. Bainton, *Erasmus of Christendom* (New York: Charles Scribner's Sons, 1969), 8–11.
4. Erasmus, *Christian Humanism*, 26–27; J. Kelley Sowards, *Desiderius Erasmus* (Boston: Twayne Publishers, 1975), 4–9.
5. Bainton, *Erasmus*, 41–43, 113–114; Johan Huizinga, *Erasmus and the Age of the Reformation* (New York: Harper and Row, 1957), 102–103; E. Harris Harbison, *The Christian Scholar in the Age of the Reformation* (New York: Charles Scribner's Sons, 1956), 70–77.
6. Erasmus, *Christian Humanism*, 7–9.
7. *Ibid.*, 96–100, 106.
8. Sowards, *Erasmus*, 35–36, 88; Bainton, *Erasmus*, 106–109.
9. P. S. Allen, *Erasmus* (Oxford: Oxford University Press, 1934), quoted in Harbison, *Christian Scholar*, 110.
10. Bainton, *Here I Stand*, 22–23, 25–27.
11. John M. Todd, *Luther: A Life* (New York: Crossroad Publishing Co., 1982), 72–79; Bainton, *Here I Stand*, 60–66.
12. *Erasmus and His Age: Selected Letters of Desiderius Erasmus*, edited by

Hans J. Hillerbrand and trans. by Marcus A. Haworth, S. J. (New York: Harper and Row, 1970), 141, 149.

13. Erasmus, *Christian Humanism*, 138–139; 146–149.
14. *Ibid.*; *Erasmus and His Age: Selected Letters*, 153, 163, 177, 182; Bainton, *Erasmus*, 160.
15. Bainton, *Erasmus*, 187–190; Sowards, *Erasmus*, 103. One German theologian put Luther's position on free will (and indeed the general Protestant one) very succinctly when he wrote: "The central point of Luther's argument lies not in the question of whether man has the ability to do what he wishes, but rather in the question of whether he can do what he should." See Werner Elert, *Morphologie des Luthertums* (Munich: Beck, 1931), Volume I, 22, quoted in G. C. Berkouwer, *Conflict Met Rome* (Kampen: J. H. Kok, 1948), 149.
16. *Erasmus and His Age*, 176.
17. *Luther's Works*, Volume 48, *Letters* I, edited and trans. by Gottfried Krodel (Philadelphia: Fortress Press, 1963), 40, 53; see Volume 49, *Letters* II (Philadelphia: Fortress Press, 1972), 44.
18. Bainton, *Erasmus*, 192.
19. Bainton, *Here I Stand*, 385.
20. See Heiko Oberman, *Luther: Man between God and the Devil*, trans. by Eileen Walliser-Schwarzbart (New Haven: Yale University Press, 1989), 12, 44–46, 49, 64, 205.

Further Reading

BAINTON, ROLAND H. *Here I Stand: A Life of Martin Luther* (Nashville: Abingdon, 1950). Old standard work, very well done.

Erasmus and His Age: Selected Letters of Desiderius Erasmus, edited by Hans J. Hillerbrand and trans. by Marcus A. Haworth, S. J. (New York: Harper and Row, 1970). Gives reader a good look at the personality of Erasmus.

HUIZINGA, JOHAN. *Erasmus and the Age of the Reformation* (New York: Harper and Row, 1957). Sympathetic account by a countryman.

TODD, JOHN M. *Luther: A Life* (New York: Crossroad Publishing Co., 1982). Thoughtful, fair work by a Roman Catholic.

CHAPTER 12

Kangxi and Louis XIV: Dynastic Rulers, East and West

To what extent can a dynastic ruler control his own fate? What is the key to successful "absolutism"?

In the world of the late seventeenth century, a comparison between Kangxi and Louis XIV is an obvious one. At opposite ends of the Eurasian land mass, these two rulers clearly stand out. In western Europe, Louis XIV (1638–1715), a member of France's Bourbon dynasty, ruled that continent's most powerful nation. In the Far East, Kangxi (1654–1722), a member of the Qing dynasty (pronounced "ching"), was emperor of China.[1] Both rulers had equally long reigns. Kangxi's years of personal rule lasted from 1669 to 1722 (fifty-three years and four major wars) while those of Louis XIV extended from 1661 to 1715 (fifty-four years and the same number of wars).

Given their longevity, it is not surprising that each man experienced personal tragedies. Son and grandsons preceded Louis XIV in death, so that a five-year-old great-grandson, Louis XV, was left as successor in 1715. Kangxi's oldest son and "heir apparent," Yinreng, was infamous for his acts of sexual depravity, sadism, and irresponsibility. After years of fatherly patience, sorrow, and cover-ups, Kangxi declared him mad and then deposed and arrested him in 1712.[2] These family problems were also political ones, for the success of dynastic government depends upon the quality of the ruler. In the Chinese case, Kangxi's fourth son, Yinzhen, proved to be a far more capable ruler than the original heir apparent would have been. The French were less fortunate: Louis XV proved to be a lazy and mistress-ridden monarch. The Qing dynasty lasted until

1911; the Bourbon dynasty collapsed in the storm of the French Revolution (1789–1799).

The great energy and determination that both Kangxi and Louis XIV displayed clearly distinguish them from their successors. Kangxi's writings frequently note the importance of hard work and attention to detail. "This is what we have to do," he wrote. "[We have to] apply ourselves to human affairs to the utmost, while remaining responsive to the dictates of Heaven. In agriculture, one must work hard in the fields *and* hope for fair weather." Louis also relished the hard work necessary to run a large state. In notes he wrote for his successor, he warned against "prolonged idleness" and advised that a regular work schedule was good for the spirit: "No satisfaction can equal that of following each day the progress of glorious and lofty undertakings and of the happiness of the people, when one has planned it all himself."[3] Both rulers felt personally responsible for the welfare of their subjects, yet both fought major wars to extend their lands and their power. Since warfare was expensive in money and lives, it was not always easy for these men to balance their need for power with their desire to improve the lives of their subjects.

This very tension between war and peace helps illuminate some of the problems facing even a conscientious autocratic, or "absolute," ruler during these last few centuries before the world was transformed forever by the industrial revolution. Neither Louis XIV nor Kangxi had to please voters or make decisions about social and economic programs with one ear cocked to a national stock market or an international monetary system. Their job was simpler—in theory anyway. It was to strengthen the power of their dynasty by maintaining the military and economic strength of their country. The precise way in which each ruler pursued this goal tells us something about China and western Europe and something of the pitfalls facing an "absolute" ruler in the days before telephones and computers.

Kangxi was a Manchu. That fact defined his political task. The warlike Manchu nomads, who lived northeast of China, had gradually increased their territory and power at the expense of the Ming dynasty, which ruled China from 1368 to 1644. In the early seventeenth century, the Manchu leader Nurhaci (1559–1626) began to transform the Manchu tribes into a modern state by curbing the power of local chiefs and by centralizing the government. His sons continued this process of consolidation, and the Manchus were thus able to conquer Beijing easily in 1644 once the last Ming emperor was defeated and committed suicide. The major problem facing Kangxi's father, who became the first emperor of the Qing dynasty, was to win support from native Chinese leaders, especially the Confucian scholars. To accomplish this he appointed two men to all top-level government positions, one a Manchu and the other a native (or Han) Chinese. Throughout his long reign, Kangxi continued this balance in making all major appointments so that native Chinese would not unduly resent their foreign leaders. This proved wise since the Manchus, while militarily superior to the Chinese in the beginning of the reign, were vastly outnumbered. To govern China successfully, a foreign dynasty had to have so much native help in ruling that it became virtually Chinese.[4]

Kangxi was only seven years old in 1661 when his father died, leaving the government to four noblemen assigned to govern on his behalf. Although Kangxi ended this regency in 1667, it was two years later before he was able to break the power of one particularly formidable regent. When the fifteen-year-old ruler acted, he did so decisively, throwing the offending overmighty subject, Oboi, into prison, where he died five years later.[5]

By acting decisively and wisely and by presenting a strong front to real or potential enemies, Kangxi strengthened his own personal power and that of his empire. His decision to maintain a strong army required that he increase its size from 185,000 in 1661 to 315,000 in 1684. To keep his troops sharp he also took up to 70,000 of them north of the Great Wall two or three times a year on hunting trips (really military maneuvers) so that they might practice archery and riding. Domestically, he supervised affairs in the provinces through loyal officials, many of whom were former Manchu army leaders who received appointments as provincial governors. In 1667 such appointees governed twenty-eight of the twenty-nine provinces. Kangxi also shrewdly conducted frequent audiences with military leaders; he believed that a general who bowed to the emperor occasionally would remain humble and "properly fearful."[6]

By the middle of his reign, Kangxi's wise choice of subordinates, realistic understanding of people, and close attention to detail reduced the danger of rebellion by unhappy Chinese subjects or discontented Manchu clan leaders. Before this happened, however, the emperor had to fight a bloody and prolonged war against three rebel leaders in the south. This war began in 1673 and lasted until 1682, in part because the emperor had trouble finding good generals. After defeating the three rebel states, Kangxi was able to add the island of Taiwan to his empire in 1684. It was more difficult to establish Chinese power firmly in the north. This took major campaigns against the Russians and against the Mongol chieftain Galdan.

Before moving to dislodge the Russians from Chinese territory along the Amur River where they had been settling since the 1650s, Kangxi made his usual careful preparations. He collected enough military supplies for a three-year war and moved Dutch-designed cannon and men trained to use them to the front. In 1685, he captured the Russian fortress at Albazin, and in 1689 the Treaty of Nerchinsk restored Chinese control in the area.[7] It took eight more years for Kangxi to defeat the western Mongol tribes led by Galdan. "Now my purpose is accomplished, my wishes fulfilled," the elated emperor wrote when a defeated Galdan committed suicide in 1697. "Isn't this the will of Heaven? I am so extremely happy!" These western victories set the stage for Chinese domination of Tibet, which began in the final years of Kangxi's reign and has lasted intermittently to our own day.[8]

Of course, external security was not enough. Dynastic rulers were obliged to keep constant and careful watch over subjects and subordinates. Kangxi did this by devising a system of palace memorials. These secret reports from agents of unquestioned loyalty to the ruler and the dynasty contained detailed information and comments, sent directly to the emperor and viewed by him alone. Their use allowed him to bypass official channels, to learn of official incompetence and would-be plots, and to quickly acquire more accurate information than that provided by the Grand Secretariat.

One of the emperor's most trusted agents was a Manchu bondservant named Cao Yin (1658–1712). This competent administrator had a classical Confucian education, and wrote poetry with his Chinese friends in his spare time; he was an ideal informant for Kangxi, who sent him to the city of Nanjing as textile commissioner in 1692. In his role as manager of imperial textile factories, Cao Yin supervised 2500 artisans and 664 looms, and he shipped quotas of silk to Beijing. In secret palace memorials written between 1697 and his death, he gave the emperor detailed information on the local harvest, problems faced by the local governor, and the "condition of the common people." Another secret memorialist sent reports to the emperor on the movements of 5923 grain boats that left Yangzhou for Beijing each year. Such information helped the emperor keep his officials honest and stop trouble before it started.[9]

Such close supervision of foodstuffs and silk production was important to a ruler who relied on a closely regulated economy. The textile factories at Nanjing, Hangchow, and Suchow were monopolies run by the government, which provided funds and established production quotas. During his reign, Kangxi tried to strengthen these government controls over trade. In 1699, for example, a statute ended private rights to purchase copper and gave the copper monopoly to merchants from the imperial household in Beijing.[10] Neither Kangxi nor his French counterpart favored "free enterprise," which they considered inefficient and foolish. In their opinion the state alone had sufficient wealth to underwrite large commercial projects. These mercantilist rulers also asked why a private citizen should get rich with money that could be going to the state and ruler. They also worried that too-wealthy subjects might be more likely to support rebellion against their rule.

One of the central features of absolutist government was the clear tendency to link the welfare of a country with the power of its ruler. If this was the case in China, which enjoyed 2000 years of unified government, it was even more so for France. There, in the absence of a long tradition of dynastic government, it was often only the strength of the ruler that prevented the kingdom from breaking into the separate provinces from which it had been created. Louis XIV learned early the need for a strong monarchy; his lesson was as important in shaping French absolutism as Kangxi's Manchu heritage was in shaping Chinese government policies.

In 1648 when Louis was ten, an uprising known as the Fronde forced his mother and her chief minister, Cardinal Mazarin, to flee Paris to avoid capture by hostile armies. Although this uprising was poorly organized and sputtered within a few years, the revolt impressed the young monarch with the need to create both the image and the reality of a strong monarchy. When Louis assumed personal rule in 1661 after the death of Mazarin, he quickly established his authority by refusing to appoint a new chief minister and by arresting Nicholas Fouquet, his extremely wealthy and corrupt finance minister. By hard work Louis soon convinced others he was the "Sun King"; his palace at Versailles was soon the envy of other European monarchs.

The challenge Louis faced was greater than that which confronted Kangxi, since the former had to create a new tradition; the Manchu ruler, on the other hand, had only to prove that his new dynasty fitted into existing Chinese traditions. For centuries the French nobility had seen the king as only "first among equals." Louis had to change all that, and he did, using some of the same methods as his Chinese contemporary as well as some unique ones.

Like Kangxi, Louis employed officials loyal to him alone. But these differed from those in China, who were members of an ancient bureaucracy. Since France lacked a traditional bureaucracy, Louis had to build a new bureaucracy on the foundation laid by his father. His objective was to create an administration that allowed him to undercut the power of the old nobility while he strengthened his power at home and abroad. In selecting officials, the young king chose people from France's middle class—men of dedication and ability such as Michel Le Tellier as secretary of state for war and Jean-Baptiste Colbert as controller-general of finance. These commoners, like the Manchu bondservants used by Kangxi, had no social or political status other than that conferred on them by their employer; they were loyal servants because they owed everything to the king.

By employing them the king was able to create a civil and military organization that freed his dynasty from dependence on the old noble families of the realm. Louis's appointment of Colbert, in particular, proved judicious. As chief financial official, Colbert attempted to create a strong, state-directed economy designed to make the king strong in France and France strong in Europe. His international goal was a favorable balance of trade. So while the Chinese were producing silk for government consumption at state factories in Nanjing, Colbert was making France as self-sufficient as possible and generating income for the king by exports abroad from government-subsidized silk works at Lyons, linen factories at Arras, and pottery works at Nevers. To curb the import of foreign products into France, Colbert convinced the king to raise tariffs [taxes on foreign goods] in 1664 and 1667.[11] The adoption by France of this mercantilist economic system was based on the belief that there was only a limited amount of wealth in the world and the country that got to it first would prosper the most. Naturally

Colbert encouraged French establishment of trading colonies overseas, and he strengthened the royal navy and merchant marine in order to make this sort of expansion more attractive. The limited success of Colbert's policies was due to their expense. The tax structure and its collection system could not generate enough revenue to meet military and civilian needs. The French farmed out tax collection to private citizens or tax farmers, who had to turn in a fixed amount of money to the king but could keep for themselves anything collected beyond that amount. Such a system encouraged graft and placed a great burden on the poor. The fact that Louis was unable to scrap this system in favor of one able to produce more revenue and greater fairness, and the fact that the nobility remained exempt from taxation, show some of the limitations on absolute monarchs in the seventeenth century.

That Louis used Le Tellier's professional army to engage in dynastic wars rather than using his limited funds to promote greater domestic prosperity shows another flaw in the system of absolutism. Dynastic wars reflected the will of a single person, and they served as the quickest path to necessary short-term prestige. Louis chose war, at first to secure glory and territory, and finally in self-defense. The War of Devolution, 1667–1668, was fought to get territory in the Spanish Netherlands (modern Belgium). It was a limited success but led to the less successful Dutch War of 1672–1678; the Dutch prevented a decisive French victory when they opened the dikes and flooded the territory around Amsterdam. The French did expand their frontiers in both wars, and they used dubious legal claims after 1678 to continue annexations along their eastern border, taking the important fortress city of Strasbourg (then in the Holy Roman Empire) in 1681.

All this, especially when combined with Louis's insufferable vanity (he offered to settle with the Dutch in 1672 if they would strike a gold medal in his honor thanking him for giving them peace),[12] naturally alarmed Louis's neighbors. When the king moved troops into Germany in 1688, he soon found himself facing a coalition of Germans, Dutch, and English. The War of the League of Augsburg lasted until 1697 and ended in a stalemate. Louis's last war, also fought against many enemies, was the War of the Spanish Succession, 1701–1713. The decision of the French king to place his grandson on the vacant Spanish throne threatened the "balance of power" in Europe by giving the Bourbon dynasty control of two major states. Louis made matters worse by refusing to promise that the two thrones would never be united. The "Sun King" was partly defeated this time. Like the earlier contests, this was a battle for overseas markets as well as political power, with the English fighting to capture French territories across the Atlantic as well as in Europe. The French did lose Nova Scotia and Newfoundland to the British in 1713 at the Peace of Utrecht. It was the prelude to further French defeats in the Americas later in the century.

In the final analysis, the wars of Louis XIV damaged his country and his dynasty as much as the wars of Kangxi had strengthened his. In Louis's defense, we should note that neither his armies nor his territorial gains were any greater than those of the Chinese emperor. His pursuit of glory and prestige was probably not as determined as that of Kangxi. The reasons Louis's absolutism was less successful than that of Kangxi are twofold: The Chinese absolutist system was much older and more firmly established than that of France; second, in the absence of strong neighbors the Chinese did not have to conduct foreign policy (the very term would have been foreign to Kangxi) in the midst of a system of rival states, each one concerned that none of the others become too strong. Kangxi did not have to establish a tradition of strong central government in the face of a hostile aristocracy. He had only to show that he, a Manchu, was fit to sit on the throne of the "Son of Heaven." In addition, Kangxi's foreign enemies were all inferior to him in strength. Finally, there was no "balance of power" in east Asia that the Chinese emperor was expected to maintain; China was the "central country" in east Asia in fact as well as in name.

All this is not to excuse Louis XIV's arrogance or errors of judgment. It was not a good idea, either politically or economically, for Louis to achieve religious unity by allowing his officials to persecute Huguenots [French Protestants] and in 1685 to revoke the Edict of Nantes, which had given them limited religious freedom. As a consequence, a significant number of Louis's most productive subjects fled to other countries, giving the king a bad image. Louis's splendid palace at Versailles did help him control the nobility by skillfully keeping them there in attendance on him. It also awed foreign monarchs and visitors. However, the "splendid isolation" of the dynasty outside of Paris alienated later Bourbon monarchs from their subjects and was one of the reasons for the collapse of the monarchy during the French Revolution. While the Chinese emperors might also be accused of "arrogance" by a Westerner (their court ceremonial, for example, was much more elaborate than that of Louis), their "arrogance" was sanctioned by centuries-long traditions. It was, we might say, an institutional rather than a personal arrogance.

It is impossible, then, to evaluate the success or failure of either of these dynasts without taking into account their cultural and historical setting. For the Chinese, Kangxi proved a blessing. After fifty years of turmoil and inefficiency, he brought his subjects a long period of decisive, sensible, efficient rule. In short he proved himself a conservative restorer of the old.[13] Louis, on the other hand, while considered a conservative by modern standards (how else could a modern student of government view an advocate of one-man rule, sanctioned by God?), was revolutionary in the context of seventeenth-century French and European history. By identifying himself with the state, he helped to shift people's attention to the state as a focus for their primary loyalty.[14] His bureaucratic innovations, and even his wars, helped the French see their country as more than a collection of provinces. Louis may not get the credit for this, but he did help pave the way for the day when the French would die for *la patrie*, the "fatherland." It is one of the ironies of French history that a chief victim of the new spirit of national unity Louis helped create was the Bourbon dynasty he had worked so hard to strengthen.

Notes

1. Kangxi (spelled K'ang-hsi in all but the most recent works) was his title, not his personal name. Chinese rulers, much like Roman Catholic popes, took a new name when they began their rule, and so Xuan Ye (this ruler's personal name) became *the* Kangxi emperor. Many historians simplify matters and avoid confusion by using the reign title or name as if it were a personal one. I do the same in this chapter.

2. Silas H. L. Wu, *Passage to Power: K'ang-hsi and His Heir Apparent, 1661–1722* (Cambridge: MA: Harvard University Press, 1979), is an excellent study of the "murderous power struggle" between Kangxi and his son; see a good short summary in Jonathan D. Spence, *The Search for Modern China* (New York: W. W. Norton, 1990), 69–71.

3. Jonathan D. Spence, *Emperor of China: Self-Portrait of K'ang-hsi* (New York: Alfred A. Knopf, 1974), 57; see also 11, 12–13, 47, 58–59, 147; Louis XIV, king of France, *Memoires for the Instruction of the Dauphin*, trans. with an introduction by Paul Sonnino (New York: Free Press, 1970), 29–30.

4. This process by which the Manchu dynasty became both powerful and Chinese is discussed in the first fifty pages of Lawrence D. Kessler, *K'ang-hsi and the Consolidation of Ch'ing Rule, 1661–1684* (Chicago: University of Chicago Press, 1976).

5. *Ibid.*, 65–73.

6. *Ibid.*, 105, 116–118; Spence, *Emperor of China*, 42–43. Governor-generals were military leaders who controlled more than one province.

7. Kessler, *K'ang-hsi*, 100–101.

8. Wu, *Passage to Power*, 65; Spence, *Search for Modern China*, 68.

9. Jonathan D. Spence, *Ts'ao Yin and the K'ang-hsi Emperor, Bondservant and Master* (New Haven: Yale University Press, 1966), 213–254.

10. *Ibid.*, 109–110.

11. Vincent Buranelli, *Louis XIV* (New York: Twayne Publishers, 1966), 72–78.

12. John B. Wolf, *Louis XIV* (New York: W. W. Norton, 1968), 224.

13. See Jonathan D. Spence, "The Seven Ages of K'ang-hsi (1654–1722)," *Journal of Asian Studies*, XXVI (February 1967), 205–211.

14. See Roland Mousnier, *Louis XIV*, trans. by J. W. Hunt (London: The Historical Association, 1973), 18–25.

Further Reading

SONNINO, PAUL (trans.). Louis XIV, king of France, *Memoires for the Instruction of the Dauphin* (New York: Free Press, 1970). Louis speaks for himself. Read with care.

SPENCE, JONATHAN D. *Emperor of China: Self-Portrait of K'ang-hsi* (New York: Alfred A. Knopf, 1974). Excellent. Brings this ruler to life.

WOLF, JOHN B. *Louis XIV* (New York: W. W. Norton, 1968). Long but readable.